the new
ADULT
JOKE
book

the new ADULT JOKE book

Johnny Sharpe

ARCTURUS

ARCTURUS

This edition published in 2009 by Arcturus Publishing Limited
26/27 Bickels Yard, 151–153 Bermondsey Street,
London SE1 3HA

ISBN: 978-1-84837-176-7
AD000018EN

Printed in the UK

CONTENTS

AAARGH!

The restaurant was packed full with diners when all of a sudden, there was a terrible commotion and a woman began to choke on a piece of food. Quick as a flash, a man ran forward, grabbed the woman and put her face-down on the floor. Then he pulled down her knickers and licked her bottom. Immediately, the woman coughed up the piece of food and stood up fully recovered. As the man walked back to his table, his companion looked at him in astonishment. "Bloody hell, I've never seen anything like that before!" he exclaimed. "That's called the Hindlick manoeuvre," the man replied.

The foreman was just wondering why one of his men was so late getting back from making a delivery, when the phone rang.

"Sorry boss," said the man. "I had a bit of an accident on the way back, I hit a pig."

"Well, just put it on the side of the road and we'll pick it up later."

"But boss, it's not dead. It just keeps squealing."

"Okay, get the rifle from the back of the truck and put it out of its misery. Then throw it in the ditch until later."

AAARGH!

Five minutes went by and the phone rang again.

"Boss, it's me. I'm still here."

"Why? Did you do as I said?"

"Yeah, I shot it and put it in the ditch, but his motorbike is still stuck under the truck!"

For the third time that week, Ben had been late home from work and his wife was sick and tired of reheating his food.

"Next time this happens," she threatened, "your dinner will be in the bin and the bed will be made up in the spare room."

"Don't worry darling," he promised, "nothing will stop me from getting home on time tonight."

True to his word, Ben left work 10 minutes early to make sure he caught the train but alas, as he was crossing the road, a double-decker bus swerved around the corner and knocked him to the ground. Fortunately, he only had cuts and bruises but he was taken to hospital for a check up and eventually arrived home three hours late.

"So much for promises!" yelled the wife. "You've done it this time."

"It wasn't my fault! I got hit by a bus!" replied Ben.

"Oh yeah!" she replied scornfully, "and that took three hours, did it?"

A man dressed in pyjamas went up to the hotel reception and asked for the key to room 402.

"I'm sorry, sir, the room's taken," came the reply.

"I know it is," replied the man impatiently, "it's mine. I just fell out of the window!"

A man drove too fast down a country lane, skidded on some black ice and ended up in a ditch. Fortunately, a farmer appeared moments later, leading a big black horse. When he saw the man's predicament, he offered to help.

"If we tie a rope around the car, I think old Black Bess here will be able to help get it out."

So they tied the rope from the horse to the car and the farmer shouted,

"Come on Starlight, pull as hard as you can!" but the horse didn't move.

Then the farmer shouted,

"Come on Silky, one, two, three. Pull!"

But still the horse didn't move. So for a third time the farmer yelled,

"OK, Dobbin, pull now."

Nothing happened. Then he called,

"Go on Black Bess, my beauty, pull hard."

This time, the horse took the strain and slowly pulled the car out of the ditch. The motorist was very grateful but also a little puzzled.

"Don't mind me asking," he said, "but why did you call the horse by all those different names?"

"Well, it's like this," explained the farmer. "Old Black Bess is blind and if she thought she was the only one pulling, she'd never have bothered trying."

The window cleaner missed his footing and plunged ten feet to the ground where he lay nursing a broken ankle.

"Quick!" shouted a passerby, "get this man a glass of water while I call an ambulance."

"Oi, mate," groaned the window cleaner, "how far do I have to fall to get a shot of whisky?"

AAARGH!

A hapless reporter was looking for something to write about when he came across a road accident. A large crowd of people had gathered round the incident and there was no way he could get to see what had happened. Then he had an idea.

"Let me through, let me through!" he called, pushing people out of the way. "I'm the victim's son."

Eventually he got to the front to find a dead donkey lying on the ground in front of the truck.

"Is that Belle's Florist?" said the man on the end of the phone, angrily.

"Yes, it is," came the reply. "How may I help you?"

"Now listen here. I'm just celebrating the launch of my new company and I get a wreath delivered saying 'Rest in Peace.' Have you any idea what a bad impression that can make?"

"Well that is bad!" said the florist, "but it's not as bad as the impression that your 'Congratulations on Your New Location' bouquet will make at that funeral."

ANIMALS

"Right, you bloody good-for-nothing horse, you lose here today and it'll be the milk round for you tomorrow morning," said the angry jockey.

The race began and by the fifth jump it was obvious that the horse was going to be an also ran. The jockey took out his whip and gave it a sharp thwack.

"Steady on there," said the horse, "I've got to be up at four o'clock in the morning."

Little Red Riding is walking through the forest on the way to meet her Grandma when she spots someone moving.

"Mr. Wolf, Mr. Wolf," she trills, "I can see you! Come out from behind that tree."

"Bugger off," he replies angrily and disappears deeper into the forest.

Moments later, Red Riding Hood spots him again.

"Mr. Wolf, Mr. Wolf!" she calls. "I can see you behind the bush."

The wolf glowers at her and runs off. A short while later she sees him hiding behind a big rock.

"I can see you, I can see you," she says, pointing her finger at him.

"Now look here," says the wolf, "who the hell are you and what are you doing in the forest?"

"I'm Little Red Riding Hood and I'm on my way to see Grandma," she replies.

"Then fuck off and do it," yelled the wolf, "and let me have a crap in peace!"

"Mummy, mummy," said the baby camel. "Why have we got big flat feet?"

"So that we can walk across the sand easier when we're trekking through the desert," she replied.

"And why have we got such thick hides?" he continued.

"That's to protect us from the desert's fierce sun," she replied.

"But why have we got long eyelashes?"

"That's to protect our eyes against sand storms."

"So mum, what the fuck are we doing in Bristol Zoo?" he said.

"Get the carriage ready," says the King to his groom. "I've just had a telegram to say the Queen is arriving home today."

So the groom polishes the carriage, grooms the horse, puts beautiful purple plumes on its harness and then notices the animal has a huge erection.

"Hey," admonishes the groom. "Who got the telegram, you or the King?"

Dirty Jake is playing poker in the saloon but the game is not going well. Every time he loses, he kicks the puppy lying underneath the table, until the poor thing is black and blue. Eventually, it comes to the final hand and Jake, now desperate to recoup some of his losses, bets all the money he has left. Alas, he loses and is so angry, he takes his gun out of its holster and shoots the poor dog in the foot. A few years later, Dirty Jake is once again playing poker in the salon when suddenly the doors fly open and in walks a huge dog, standing on his hind legs, he's over six feet tall. The bar goes quiet as the dog takes out a gun and growls,

"I'm looking for the man that shot my paw."

ANIMALS

The ancient Roman animal trainer released the lions into the Colosseum, and turned to his assistant with a sigh.

"They're a poor lot, this week," he said glumly, "even worse than the ones last year."

"I know," replied his assistant, "the Christians aren't up to much either, are they?"

"No," said the trainer. "Bloody awful shower."

"Still, look on the bright side," said his assistant, "at least we don't get pitch invasions like they do at the chariot races."

Two snakes are creeping through the undergrowth when one says to the other:

"What kind of snakes are we? Do we kill our prey by squeezing them to death or give them a bite of our deadly poison?"

"We're the poisonous ones," replied the second snake, "why do you ask?"

"Because I've just bitten my lip."

When the away team turned up for the match, they were amazed to see that the goalkeeper for the opposing side was a Great Dane. The dog performed incredibly and stopped the away team scoring.

After the match, the away Captain asked the opposing team how they ever managed to get the dog to play so well.

"Well, it's the same for everyone," replied the manager, "practise, practise, practise."

A young soldier was sent to a remote outpost deep in the desert. After 3 months, he awoke one morning to loud cheers and the banging of drums.

"What's happening?" he asked his colleague.

"The goat herd is passing through again. Someone's spotted them on the horizon and is letting everyone know. Come on or we'll be late."

The newest recruit was hurried along and pushed through the fort gates.

"But why is everyone rushing?" he exclaimed. "There's still plenty of time before they get here."

"Maybe," replied his friend, "but if you're too late, all the good looking ones have gone."

"Welcome home, Brian!" said the banner over the pub door as the intrepid explorer returned from his safari in darkest Africa. After a few pints, his crowd of well-wishers asked him to tell them some of his more hair-raising stories.

Brian sat back and began:

"There was this one day when I went out alone into the jungle and strayed into unknown territory. Suddenly I heard a loud roar behind me and turning round, I saw a huge lion ready to pounce. Well, I just ran for it. Luckily, just as it was about to get me, it slipped and I was able to run on. But next moment, he was breathing down my neck again. Then just as I thought it was curtains, he slipped again and I managed to run back into the camp."

His audience listened spellbound until a voice from the back remarked,

"Bloody hell, Brian, if that had been me, I'd have shit my pants."

Brian turned to the speaker and replied,

"What do you think the lion kept slipping on?"

A boy was crossing the road one day when a frog called out to him and said, "If you kiss me, I'll turn into a beautiful princess."

The boy bent over, picked up the frog, put it in his pocket and carried on walking. The frog spoke up again, "If you kiss me and turn me back into a beautiful princess I will stay with you for one week." But the boy just carried on walking.

The frog was desperate by this time and so cried out, "If you kiss me and turn me back into a beautiful princess, I'll stay with you forever and do ANYTHING you want!" But the boy just kept going.

Finally the frog asked, "What's the matter? I've told you I'm beautiful, willing, and will stay with you forever. Why won't you kiss me?"

And the boy replied, "I'm a software engineer, and I find girls kinda weird. But a talking frog? Now that's cool…"

The hedgehog made his way down the riverbank and very slowly walked into the water. As it got deeper, he soldiered on, gasping for breath. Suddenly he disappeared under and was only just able to get back to the bank.

After resting quietly for 10 minutes, the hedgehog tried again; after going under twice more he managed to get back to dry land before collapsing. This time it took him much longer to recover but once he felt fit enough, he started back into the water. Two ducks were watching from the other side of the bank and one said to the other:

"Come on George, don't you think it's time we told him he was adopted?"

A woman arrived home from work to discover her dog had the next door neighbour's hamster in its mouth. Horrified, she ordered the dog to drop it but the poor little creature was well and truly dead.

"Oh damn!" she cursed, "what will Mr Jones say about this!"

Then she had a great idea. She took the hamster inside, bathed it and combed its fur then crept quietly next door and put the animal back in its cage.

Some days passed before she met up with her neighbour and as they chatted, the hamster came up in conversation.

"You won't believe this," said Mr Jones, "but a week ago our hamster died and we buried him in the garden."

"Oh really?" replied the woman.

"Yes, but some sick bugger dug him up and put him back inside his cage!"

A Texan farmer goes to Australia for a vacation. There he meets an Aussie farmer and gets talking. The Aussie shows off his big wheat field and the Texan says, "Oh! We have wheat fields that are at least twice as large."

Then they walk around the ranch a little, and the Aussie shows off his herd of cattle. The Texan immediately says, "We have longhorns that are at least twice as large as your cows."

The conversation has, meanwhile, almost died when the Texan sees a herd of kangaroos hopping through the field. He asks, "And what are those?"

The Aussie replies with an incredulous look, "Don't you have any grasshoppers in Texas?"

A game of poker was being played on a bench in the park and a passer-by was amazed to see that one of the players was a dog. As he stopped to watch, the dog won three hands in a row.

"Wow!" he exclaimed, "that's fantastic. I've never seen such a clever dog."

One of the other players replied,

"Oh, he's not that clever. Whenever he gets a good hand, he wags his tail."

A woman walked past a pet shop on the way to work and outside on a perch was a beautiful parrot. As she passed by, he squawked loudly,

"Oh, Madam, you are so ugly."

Upset, the woman hurried on, but the next day as she passed the shop, he called out loudly

"Madam, madam, you are so ugly," causing other passers-by to look at her with interest.

After enduring this humiliation for a week, she could take it no longer. She walked angrily into the shop and confronted the manager.

"Any more abuse from that parrot and I'll wring its neck," she raged.

The owner promised it wouldn't happen again and when she passed the following morning, she looked for any reaction from the bird. Silence, but as she reached the corner:

"Oh, Madam, Madam… you know, don't you?"

Dave was early for his date with Sonia so while she went off to get ready, he started to play with her little dog on the living room carpet. He found a ball and began throwing it around the room for the dog to chase. However, he got a little over-enthusiastic and

the ball flew out of the open door onto the 10th floor balcony and over the railings to the ground below. The dog followed.

Stunned, Dave just sat there until his girlfriend appeared.

"Erm… Sonia," he said hesitantly, "have you noticed how depressed your dog has become recently?"

A man had been crossing the desert by camel for over three months. Lacking any female company, he suddenly had a most awful urge – one that had to be satisfied straight away. He backed the camel over to a pile of rocks, stood on top of the rocks and undid his flies. Alas, as he moved towards the animal, it walked further away. Undaunted, he backed up the camel again and got on top of the rocks but once more the animal walked a few feet away.

This farce went on for another fifteen minutes or so, when out of the blue appeared a gorgeous young girl.

"I can't believe it," he said as he looked her up and down. "I say," he continued, smiling with satisfaction, "would you mind holding the camel for me?"

ANIMALS

David received a parrot for his birthday. This parrot was fully grown with a bad attitude and worse vocabulary. Every other word was an expletive. Those that weren't expletives were, to say the least, rude.

David tried hard to change the bird's attitude and was constantly saying polite words, playing soft music; anything that came to mind. Nothing worked. He yelled at the bird, the bird got worse. He shook the bird and the bird got madder and ruder.

Finally, in a moment of desperation, David put the parrot in the freezer. For a few moments he heard the bird squawking, kicking and screaming and then, suddenly, all was quiet.

David was frightened that he might have actually hurt the bird and quickly opened the freezer door.

The parrot calmly stepped out onto David's extended arm and said: "I'm sorry that I offended you with my language and actions. I ask for your forgiveness. I will try to check my behaviour..."

David was astounded at the bird's change in attitude and was about to ask what changed him when the parrot continued, "May I ask what the chicken did?"

ANIMALS

A dog was terrorising the neighbourhood.

"If you don't keep him under better control, he'll have to be taken away," the owner was told, so they had him neutered.

However, on the following day the postman was walking up the garden path when the dog jumped out and sunk his jaws deep into the man's leg.

"Get him off, get him off!" yelled the postman as the owner rushed out to drag the dog away.

"I'm so sorry," apologised the owner. "I can't understand why he's still so aggressive; I've just had him neutered."

"Well you should have had all his teeth taken out instead," retorted the postman angrily. "As soon as I saw him I knew he wasn't going to screw me."

"Oh Jack," said mum, "our Julie wants to take the dog for a walk but the dog's on heat."

"Don't worry," replied dad, "I know what to do about that." He went into the garage and doused a cloth with some petrol, which he then rubbed all over the dog's bum. "That'll disguise the smell, so the dogs won't be attracted," he said. However, 40 minutes later the daughter returned without the dog.

"Where's the dog?" asked her parents anxiously.

"We ran out of fuel half way round," replied Julie, "but it's okay, there's a big Alsatian pushing her home."

Two men were boasting about their dogs.

"Mine can carry out four orders all at the same time," said the first man. "Watch, I'll show you."

"Rover, pop down the paper shop, get me the Racing Post and on the way back pick up a betting slip and a pen from the bookies. Oh, and pick up last week's winnings."

Sure enough, the dog arrived back 10 minutes later with everything the man asked for.

"Very good," said the second man, "but watch this... Springer, get me some food."

The dog disappeared and arrived back 15 minutes later with an egg and a saucepan of water. He gathered together some sticks, lit a fire and placed the saucepan of water on top of it. When the water boiled, he put in the egg and then stood on his head.

"That's fantastic," remarked the first man, "but why is he standing on his head?"

"Because he broke the eggcup last week," came the reply.

A woman had a beautiful carpet but it was badly stained because her dog kept peeing all over it. So she cut out the stains and took the pieces along to the carpet shop.

"I'm no fool," she said. "Can I have a carpet the colour of these stains, please."

A woman was in the cinema when she noticed a man and his dog sitting in front of her. The dog was glued to the screen. He would cry at the sad bits and bark joyously when it was funny.

After the film was over, she tapped the man on the shoulder and commented on his remarkable dog.

"Yes, I'm amazed at his reaction," replied the man, "because he didn't like the book at all."

One day the beautiful princess was walking through the woods when she came across a frog sitting on a lily pad.

"Good day to you," said the frog, "do not be alarmed. I am really a handsome prince who was turned into a frog by a wicked old witch. If you kiss me, I will turn back into my former self and we can live happily ever after. We'll get married and live in a mighty castle. You can set up home, learn to cook, wash my clothes and have my children."

Later that night, the princess sat down to a plate of frog's legs lightly sautéed in white wine and onions. She looked at it and smiled.

"I don't think so," she said.

ARISTOCRATS

First and foremost, Sir Henry Pennington was a true aristocrat who believed in a stiff upper lip, true patriotism and right and proper etiquette.

One night he returned early from his club to discover his eldest daughter writhing around on the floor with a young earl.

"Dorothy!" he yelled, "let's do it right! Arch your back immediately and lift that gentleman's balls off the cold floor."

The butler was very keen to impress his new employers so he was working hard to stay alert to all the guests' wishes. Suddenly, as a female guest leant over to reach for the salt, her tits fell out of her low-cut dress. Quick as a flash, the butler picked up two serving spoons and placed them back inside her dress before anyone had noticed what had happened. Later that night, as the final guests left, the host turned to his butler and commended him on his quick thinking.

"But I think if it happens again, a warm spoon may be more acceptable."

Lady Matilda only had a dressing gown on when her butler entered unannounced to tell her that the guests were arriving.

"Henry!" she scolded, "You must knock and wait for me to answer before you come into my bedroom. For all you know, I may have just got out of the bath."

"No need to worry, ma'am," replied Henry, "I always look through the keyhole before I come in."

On another occasion, Lady Highbrow was forced to sack her cook.

"It's no good, Dorothy, you are unable to maintain the standards I expect. Your cooking is boring and the state of the kitchen is a disgrace."

"Well, good riddance to this flaming job," retorted the cook. "Not everyone in this house thinks I'm bad. Your husband says I do a great coq au vin and what's more, I'm better in bed than you are."

"What!" roared Lady Highbrow. "Who told you that? My husband?"

"No, the gardener!"

ARISTOCRATS

What's your idea of a perfect husband?

A peer of the realm with a £1 million life insurance who dies on his wedding night.

Lady Snooks rang the bell to summon the footman to her bedroom.

"James, take off my dress." The footman did so.

"James, take off my bra." Again, the footman did as he was asked.

"James, take off my, ahem, underthings." James duly complied.

"And now, James, if I ever find you wearing any of my clothes again, you shall be instantly dismissed!"

BAND AID

A man joins a group of war veterans listening to a brass band in the park. All of a sudden the man in front of him begins to twitch his head backwards and forwards in sudden jerky movements.

"I'm sorry," he says, "it's an old injury I got from the war."

A few moments later, the man to the left of him begins to throw his arms around in the air.

"Sorry," he gasps, "can't help it. I got it in the war."

Then the man on his right starts to shake his hand about, faster and faster it goes.

"Did you get that in the war as well?" he asks.

"No," comes the reply. "I got it from my nose and now I can't get it off my finger."

BARS

A customer walks up the bar and attracts the barman's attention.

"Can I have a packet of helicopter-flavour crisps, please?" he asks.

"Sorry, mate," says the barman, "we've only got plane."

"Bloody women!" cursed the man at the bar. "I think my wife is having an affair with a travelling salesman. Last night I found a case of brushes under the bed!"

"Yeah, bloody women," agreed the bartender. "I think my wife's having an affair with a pet shop owner. When I got home, I found two budgies, 1 parrot and three gerbils under our bed."

A man further down the bar had been listening to this conversation and he spoke up.

"That's nothing, I think my wife's having an affair with a horse. I came home last night and found a jockey under our bed!"

BARS

A man walked up to a bar and the landlord said,

"Sir, you know you've got a steering wheel shoved down your trousers?"

"I know," replied the man. "It's driving me nuts!"

A shepherd's pie walks up to the bar and orders a pint of bitter.

"Sorry, mate," says the barman, "we don't serve food in here."

A stranger walks into a crowded bar and asks for a pint of beer. As he stands sipping it, someone suddenly shouts out '53' and the whole pub collapses in laughter. Someone else calls '46' and the crowd bursts into further merriment.

"Hey, what's going on?" asks the stranger.

The bartender replies,

"It's a local crowd in here and because everyone knows each other, they don't bother to tell their jokes anymore, they just call out the number of their joke."

"I see," says the stranger, and later when there's a sudden lull in the laughter, he calls out '19'.

There's a hushed silence. Bewildered, the stranger calls out '51'. Again there's no reaction. He turns to the bartender in amazement.

"I don't understand," he says, "Why aren't they laughing?"

The bartender gives a knowing shake of the head.

"Ah well, you see, it's the way you tell them."

After downing his 12th pint, the man's mood changed from happy to quarrelsome. Suddenly, he stood up and shouted to everyone in the room.

"Alright, you tossers! Everyone on this side of the room is a dirty bastard and everyone on that side is queer."

The room went quiet as everyone stared at him in astonishment. And then a man quietly got up and walked to the other side of the room.

"Where the hell are you going?" demanded the drunk, "looking for trouble, are you?"

"No, no," replied the man hastily, "it's just that I'm on the wrong side of the room."

BARS

Two men, off the oilrigs, arrive back in Aberdeen and head for the nearest bar. They order two pints of heavy and two whisky chasers which they down in a couple of minutes. Another round of drinks is ordered and then another five minutes later, followed by a third round five minutes after that. After the next round of drinks are placed in front of them, one man turns to his mate, lifts his glass and says 'Cheers!'

The other man replies impatiently,

"Hey, did we come here for a drink or just to talk crap all night?"

A stranger was sitting morosely at the end of the bar, staring into his pint of beer.

"Looks like you've got the whole world on your shoulders," remarked the barman sympathetically. "Are you alright?"

The stranger looked up sadly and replied,

"It's the curse of the drink. Booze makes you angry. It makes you want to pick a fight. It makes you want to shoot your wife. It makes you miss!"

A woman goes into a bar and asks for a double entendre.

So the barman gives her one.

A man walked into a bar and saw a sign that said 'ham sandwiches £2.50, cheese sandwiches £2.00, hand job £12.'

"Do you do the hand jobs?" he asked the girl behind the bar.

"Yes," she said.

"Well, wash your hands and get me a cheese sandwich," he replied.

"What's up, Steve?" asked the barman. "You're looking a bit pissed off."

"I am," replied Steve. "I just passed that new sperm bank that's opened round the corner and it's paying £25 for every sample."

He shook his head sadly. "I've let a fortune run through my fingers!"

BIMBOS

A blonde goes into a hotel room and it's more than 3 hours before she comes out again.

"What happened to you?" asks her friend. "We all had dinner ages ago."

"I couldn't get out," she replies. "There were 3 doors in the room, one went into the bathroom, one into the wardrobe and the third had a 'do not disturb' notice hanging on the door."

A blonde was giving details of a car accident she'd had the day before.

"Now miss, can you tell me what gear you were in at the time of the collision?"

"Oh yes," she replied, "a beautiful blue trouser suit with matching shoes and handbag in navy blue."

What's the difference between an ironing board and a blonde?

It's hard to open the legs of an ironing board.

BIMBOS

What do you get when you turn three blondes upside down?

Three brunettes.

A student goes to a young professor's office. She glances down the hall, closes his door, kneels down and pleads:

"I would do anything to pass this exam."

She leans closer to him, flips back her hair, gazes meaningfully into his eyes, "I mean," she whispers, "I would do anything..."

He returns her gaze, "Anything?"

"Anything."

His voice softens, "Anything?"

"Anything!" she repeats.

His voice turns to a whisper.

"Would you... study?"

A brunette was walking down the middle of the road saying 74 to herself over and over again. A blonde spotted her and called out,

"What are you doing?"

"Don't you know?" replied the brunette. "It's great fun. You should try it."

So the blonde walked into the middle for the road and began chanting '74, 74,74…'

Suddenly, a lorry appeared and knocked her down. The brunette continued,

"75, 75, 75…"

A blonde got stuck in some quicksand and it wasn't long before only her head and shoulders were left above the ground. Fortunately, one of the strongest men from the local village was passing by and he heard the blonde's cries for help.

"Don't panic!" he called, "just grab my hand and I'll soon pull you out."

But no matter how hard he pulled, the poor blonde just sank lower and lower.

"I can't understand it," said the strongman. "I'll have to go and get some help."

"No wait," shouted the blonde in panic. "Would it help if I took my feet out of the stirrups?"

A ventriloquist is doing his act at the summer show and telling a few blonde jokes. Suddenly, a blonde woman stands up at the back and shouts out angrily,

"You bastard, it's always the same, telling everyone that blondes are stupid. Well, we're not."

"Look, I'm sorry," says the ventriloquist, apologetically. "It's just the act; I didn't mean to…"

"I'm not talking to you," interrupts the blonde heatedly, "it's that little bastard on your knee who's telling all the jokes!"

BRAINLESS

"Doctor, doctor," said the anguished man. "I can't satisfy my wife in bed any more, what shall I do?"

The doctor sent him along to see an alternative healer who specialised in helping couples with this type of problem.

"When you're making love," he was told, "the healer will wave a fan above your heads and this will help stimulate your wife into having an orgasm."

So the scene was set for the following evening. As the healer waved the fan, the couple did their bit, but alas the woman remained unsatisfied. Heartbroken, the embarrassed husband said to the healer, "I bet you couldn't do any better!", so they changed places and as the husband waved the fan, the couple writhed beneath him. In no time at all the woman had a marvellous orgasm, and the husband said bitterly,

"You see, that's how you're supposed to wave the fan!"

Sherlock Holmes and Dr. Watson went on a camping trip. As they lay down for the night, Holmes said: "Watson, look up into the sky and tell me what you see."

Watson said, "I see millions and millions of stars."

Holmes: "And what does that tell you?"

Watson: "Astronomically, it tells me that there are millions of galaxies and potentially billions of planets. Theologically, it tells me that God is great and that we are small and insignificant. Meteorologically, it tells me that we will have a beautiful day tomorrow. What does it tell you?"

Holmes: "That somebody stole our tent."

Three hillbillies walked into a fast food restaurant and took a table by the window. One of them drew his friends' attention to a sign above the counter and the next moment, they all had their todgers out, wanking away as fast as possible. The waitress came over and looked at them in amazement.

"What the hell do you think you're doing?" she demanded.

They replied, "We saw the sign up there saying 'first come, first served' and we're starving."

Three men were chatting in the pub and the conversation turned to children.

"We were going to call our son Gerald," said the first man, "but he was born on April 23 so we called him George, after St. George."

"Well, that's a coincidence," said the second man, "because our son was born on St. David's Day, so we called him David."

"Would you believe it!" exclaimed the Irishman. "The same thing happened with my son, Pancake!"

Patrick and Stan are walking down the lane when they see Molloy swimming around in a field of grass.

"Now look at that," remarks Patrick, "what a stupid bugger, have you ever seen anything so silly. He shouldn't be there."

"Don't you think you ought to go and get him?" says Sean.

"I would," replies Patrick, "only I can't swim!"

Three simple men scooped the prizes in the local raffle. The first won a crate of beer, the second won a side of pork and the third won the booby prize, a toilet brush. The following week they met for a drink and the first remarked,

"Well, that was a bit of luck last week, I really enjoyed my beer."

"Yes, indeedy," said the second man, nodding his head, "the pork was great, especially the crackling."

"And what about you?" they said, looking at the third man.

"Well, I was a bit disappointed, to be honest," he replied. "I think I'll just go back to using paper."

An Englishman, a Scotsman and an Irishman escape from Dartmoor Prison and disappear into the surrounding countryside, hotly pursued by a group of prison officers with tracker dogs.

"Quick!" whispers the Englishman. "If we don't do something soon, those dogs are going to hunt us down. Get up a tree as soon as you can."

The Englishman scrambles up a beech tree and lies very still. Suddenly, there's an excited barking of dogs and the prison officers burst through the undergrowth and surround the tree.

"I think there's something up there!" one of officers says excitedly.

"Hey, who's up there?" he yells.

The Englishman mimics the sound of a pigeon.

"Damn, it's only a bird," they say, and leave disappointed.

Moments later, the dogs start barking again and surround another tree.

"Who's up there?" shout the officers.

The Scotsman, hiding in the branches, calls 'twit twoo, twit twoo.'

"A bloody owl," they grumble and continue on their way. Then for a third time the dogs start barking frantically.

"Right, gotcha!" shouts one of the officers. "Who's up there?"

The Irishman replies, "Moo, moo…"

Did you hear about Marvin, the actor?

He cut his leg off to play Long John Silver. He didn't get the part though. He had the wrong leg amputated.

"Bob!" called the newspaper editor, "did you go and check out that story about the woman who could sing soprano and alto at the same time?"

"Yeah," replied Bob. "But there was no story. The woman had two heads."

Said the weak wally to his wife,

"Now come on dear, the boss is being very fair. He said he'd really like to give me the day off, but if he did, then he'd have to do it for everyone whose wife had just given birth to sextuplets!"

Two simple men decide to go on a weekend fishing trip. They pop down to the local store and get fully kitted out with all the right gear for good weather and bad... plus hundreds of pounds worth of fishing tackle and camping equipment.

After fishing for two days on the bank of the river, they manage to catch just one small fish between them.

"Bloody hell!" exclaims one, "that damned fish has cost us nearly £1,000."

"Well then," says the other, "it's a good thing we didn't catch anymore!"

Two simple men park up outside the cinema and jump out of the car. They've just closed the doors when the driver curses,

"Bloody hell, I've left the keys in the car and the door's locked."

"Well, let's call the garage," said the other.

"No, that's no good. All the phones round here are broken."

"OK, let's smash a window."

"Oh no, I couldn't bear to do that, it'll cost a fortune."

"Well you'd better hurry up and think of something 'cos it's beginning to rain and the hood's down!"

Two simple-minded men stopped for a meal at a motorway cafe and discovered it was running a special competition. If you picked the correct number from that day's menu, you won a session of free sex.

"Come on Jake, let's have a go!" urged Dan.

"I'll have number 14, the tomato soup," said Dan, "and my mate will have number 5, egg and chips."

The waiter took down the order and looked at their expectant faces.

"I'm sorry," he said shaking his head, "you've picked the wrong numbers."

During the following two weeks, the men went back on six occasions but failed every time to pick the winner.

"I think this whole competition is a fake!" complained Jake on his seventh try.

"Oh no," replied Dan, "it's on the level. My wife won twice last week."

CHEMIST

A man walked into a chemist shop and asked the feisty young salesgirl for one hundred condoms.

"Well fuck me!" she exclaimed.

"In that case, make it 101," he replied.

A man went into the chemist shop and asked for a deodorant.

"Will that be the ball type?" asked the assistant.

"No, underarm, please," replied the man.

"Do you sell extra large condoms?" the woman asked the chemist.

"Yes we do," he said, "would you like a packet?"

"No thanks, but do you mind if I wait here until somebody does?"

CHURCH

A man emigrated to America sixty years ago and accumulated great wealth. Upon his death the rich man's will stipulated that his hundred million pound bequest was to be divided equally among his three closest friends: Smith, Jones and Green. There was only one small provision: each of the heirs was required to deposit one hundred thousand pounds in the coffin before it was lowered into the ground. This act, according to the deceased's statement, was to prove their good faith while the will was in probate.

As the coffin was about to be closed for the last time, Jones quickly deposited his hundred thousand pounds into the casket. Green followed suit and placed his hundred thousand pounds besides Jones's money. Then Smith reached into the coffin, withdrew the two hundred thousand pounds in cash and replaced it with a cheque for three hundred thousand pounds.

A rich man moved into the neighbourhood and went to church on the Sunday morning where he listened to a spellbinding sermon. After the service was over, he took the vicar by the hand and shook it vigorously.

"That was the best damned sermon I've ever heard," he said forcefully.

"Well thank you very much," replied the vicar, somewhat taken aback by the man's enthusiasm.

"But erm… I'd rather you didn't curse," he said.

The rich man continued,

"Yes, you can count on me to be at this service every week, it was bloody marvellous."

"Good, good," replied the vicar, "but please don't swear."

"In fact, it was so damned great, I put £1,000 in the collection," he added.

"Fuck me!" said the vicar.

After Sunday service, the vicar greeted his congregation as they left the church. Last to leave was Martha who was obviously quite distressed.

"Martha, my dear, what's wrong?" he asked, looking concerned.

"It's my husband," she replied, sobbing, "he's dead."

"I'm sorry to hear that!" said the vicar. "Did he say anything before he died? What were his last words?"

"Put that gun down," she replied.

CHURCH

A churchman was celebrating 25 years in the parish and as a special thank you, the congregation arranged for him to spend two weeks in Florida. He arrived at the hotel and was shown to his room where he found a naked girl lying across the bed. Immediately, he rang up his parish and told them how angry he was at what they had done. On hearing this, the girl got up to go but the man said quickly, "Hold on, I'm angry at them, I'm not angry at you."

COMPANY MATTERS

John was only 19 when he suffered terrible injuries that left him without any ears. He was determined to become successful despite the disability and by the time he was 40 he had built up a prestigious, world-renowned company and was a millionaire many times over.

The time came when he needed a good 'right hand' man so from all the applications received, he whittled it down to 3.

The first man was interviewed and showed great business acumen. John was impressed. However at the end of the interview he asked the final, important question.

"Do you notice anything different about me?"

"You've got no ears," came the reply.

Poor John, he was so touchy about his appearance that he dismissed the man immediately.
The second candidate was interviewed and she was even more impressive than the first. Then he came to the final question. "And how would you describe me?" he asked.

"You've got no ears," she replied, so she didn't get the job either.

So it came to the third person. The man strode in confidently and did a perfect interview. John was extremely impressed. He asked the final question.

"And what about me, is there anything you notice?"

"Yes," replied the man "you wear contact lenses."

John was overjoyed. "That's right, how did you know?"

"Because it would be hard to wear glasses without any fucking ears," answered the man.

Morris had just been hired as the new CEO of a large, high-tech corporation. The CEO who was stepping down met with him privately and presented him with three numbered envelopes... #1,#2,#3.

"Open one of these if you run up against a problem you don't think you can solve, and good luck." the departing CEO said.

Six months later, sales took a downturn and Morris was really catching a lot of heat. Nearly at his wits' end he remembered the envelopes.

He went to his drawer and at the back, almost forgotten, he found them. He took out the first envelope. The message read, "Put all the blame on your predecessor."

So Morris called a press conference and tactfully laid the blame at the feet of the previous CEO. Satisfied with his comments, the press – and Wall Street – responded positively, sales began to pick up and the problem was soon behind him.

About a year later, the company was again experiencing a dip in sales, combined with serious product problems. Having learned from his previous experience, the CEO quickly opened the second envelope. The message read, "Reorganize."

This he did, and the company quickly rebounded.

After several consecutive profitable quarters, the company once again fell on difficult times. Morris went to his office, closed the door and opened the third envelope.

The message said, "Prepare three envelopes."

A builder was at the top of a high scaffold, when he realised he needed a saw. Two floors below him, he spotted his mate so he called to him.

"Pete!" he hollered. "I" he said, pointing to his eye, "need" he continued, pointing to his knee, "a saw" he finished, making a sawing movement with his hands.

But then to his astonishment, his mate took out his

willy and began masturbating. So quickly, the builder came down to where his mate was standing and said, "Bill, what the hell are you doing?"

"I was just letting you know I was coming," replied his mate, innocently.

A man was walking along the street with two screaming babies under his arm.

"Dear me!" exclaimed a passer-by. "They must be hungry, why don't you feed them? You can't be much of a father."

"Listen lady," said the man impatiently. "I'm not their father. I'm a condom salesman and I'm taking these two complaints back to the company."

The general manager of a local company prided himself on knowing what was going on with the workforce. However, one evening he returned home from work in a foul mood.

"What's wrong?" asked his wife.

"Bloody Jenkins, in packing," he replied. "Asked for the afternoon off to go to his uncle's funeral. Well, I wasn't having that. I thought it was the old trick to get to see the football match, so I followed him."

"So what happened? Did your team lose?" "What team? It was his uncle's bloody funeral!"

A delivery truck arrives at the gates of a science laboratory and the driver is directed to a building on the far side of the factory site.

"I've got a batch of cages outside for you," he tells the scientist, "where shall I put them?"

The scientist points to a separate room and is just walking away when the deliveryman calls to him, "What do you want all these cages for?"

"We're going to be keeping some lawyers in them," the scientist replies. "They're going to be used for tests."

The deliveryman scratches his head in puzzlement: "Don't you normally use rats for that?"

"Yeah, but we get so attached to rats."

COMPANY MATTERS

An English businessman was invited to a state banquet while on a visit to Moscow. He was sitting next to a stunning blonde who smiled warmly at him as he sat down. Halfway through the meal, having drunk a few vodkas, he knocked his napkin on the floor and fondled the girl's ankle as he picked it up but the girl did not react. A little later, the man dropped his knife and this time when he picked it up, he fondled the girl's knee. Again, there was no reaction. But then suddenly, as his hand moved further up her leg, she began scribbling furiously on the back of her serviette, which she passed over to him.

It read, "When you get to where you want to be, please show no surprise, whatsoever. Yours sincerely, Arthur St. John Parkinson, MI5."

The managing director rose to his feet and glared at the men sitting round the boardroom table.

"Right!" he demanded, "who's been having an affair with my secretary?"

The room went silent.

"Okay," continued the M.D, "who hasn't had an affair with my secretary?"

Again, there was silence and then a hand was slowly raised.

"Actually sir, I haven't," said a small, shaky voice.

"In that case, you sack her," ordered the M.D.

A girl came out of the interview room looking very pleased with herself.

"I think I've got the job," she told the receptionist, "there's only one other person waiting."

"Well, let me just give you a word of warning," replied the receptionist, "your new boss thinks he'd God's gift to women. He'll have you over the desk, ripping your dress off, in less than an hour."

"Thanks for the tip," she replied, "I'll just have to make sure I'm wearing old clothes."

The managing director called for his chief accountant.

"Andrew, I'm very disappointed," he said. "I have a report in front of me here, describing your disgraceful behaviour at the office party last night. It says, and I quote, Andrew was seen dancing naked around a tree in the company courtyard. Tied to the tree was another man singing at the top of his voice! Now, what have you to say for yourself? What were you doing?"

"Well, you ought to know," retorted Andrew. "You were the one tied to the tree!"

A very obese man had been dieting for three months but one day he arrived at work carrying a huge jam and double cream doughnut. His work friends admonished him.

"Come on Bill, you're on a diet, you shouldn't be having that."

Bill replied, "It was just meant to be. This morning, as I drove to work, I saw this doughnut in the baker shop and I thought to myself, if there's a parking place nearby then it's God's wish that I should have it. And guess what, after driving round 10 times, there was a parking place!"

A woman was drinking in the company bar when 3 of her male colleagues came to join her.

"Damn this bloody audit," said one. "I'm really screwed."

"Me too," said another. "I'm bloody screwed as well."

The third man shook his head in despair.

"And I'm really fucked," he said sorrowfully.

In the silence that followed, the woman said,

"Hey, guys, can you tell me how I can get audited?"

CONFESSIONALS

The priest had been in his new parish for 18 months and already he was fed up with the number of people coming to him in confession and talking about their affairs. Eventually he told his congregation to use another word.

"From now on, I would like you to say you have fallen, instead of telling me you're having an affair," he said.

The new word worked well. Then it came to the priest's summer holiday and another priest came to stand in for a month but was not made aware of the new arrangement. After 2 weeks of listening to the daily confessions, he was astonished at what he was being told so he went to see the Lord Mayor.

"I'm very pleased with the local people's morals," he said. "They have very little to confess to me. I think something should be done about the state of the pavements, though, because people seem to be falling down all the time."

The Lord Mayor smiled, knowingly.

"Oh, there's nothing to worry about there, Father," he replied.

"Well I think there is," persisted the priest. "Your wife has fallen 3 times this week."

CONFESSIONALS

"Forgive me Father, for I have sinned," said the man in the confessional.

"What is it my son?"

"During the war I hid a resistance fighter in my attic."

"But that's not a sin. That's a very courageous act," said the priest.

"But I charged him 20 francs every week of his stay."

"Hmm," mused the priest. "That's not something to be proud about, but at least you risked your life and saved his."

"Just one more thing," continued the man, "do you think I ought to tell him the war's over?"

"Forgive me Father for I have sinned," said the man in the confessional.

"What is it, my son?" came the reply.

"Well, last week I went round to my girlfriend's flat but she wasn't in. The only person there was her flat mate and we ended up having sex."

"Oh dear," replied the priest.

"And then a couple of days later, I popped round to my mate's house but he'd gone down the pub. The only person there was his wife and we ended up having sex."

"Oh dear," remarked the priest again.

The man continued

"So then last night, I went into the local pub and it was empty. Everyone had gone to watch the darts team playing away. There was only Mandy serving behind the bar so we ended up having sex. What shall I do?"

But there was no answer from the other side of the screen.

"Father, are you there?" demanded the man. No answer came, so he began looking for the priest and eventually found him hiding in the pews.

"What are you doing there?" he exclaimed.

"Well, I suddenly realised that you and I were alone together," replied the priest.

COUPLES

It was Friday night and Bob was down the pub with his mate Pete.

"Going to the match tomorrow?" asked Bob

"Oh, I dunno," replied Pete, "my wife's not keen on me being out every Saturday."

"Listen, that's no problem. On Saturday morning, take her upstairs, strip her naked and give her the best shagging you can. When she's really enjoying herself then tell her you're going to the match."

On Monday, the two men met up for a lunchtime pint. "Didn't see you on Saturday," remarked Bob, "did you try what I said?"

"Yeah!" replied Pete. "I took the wife upstairs, ripped her clothes off, saw her lying there on the bed and thought 'Oh bugger it, the team's not been playing that well anyway'!"

A couple were at the cinema.

"Are you comfortable there?" he asked her.

"Yes thanks," she replied.

"I hope the seat's not torn and covered in crumbs," he continued.

"Oh no, it's fine," she said.

"And have you got a good view?" he persisted.

"Yes, it's fine," she replied.

"Great," said her date. "Swap seats."

The unfaithful husband went to pick up his wife Connie from a conference and was startled to see her leaving the building with his mistress. He hid from sight until his mistress had gone, then picked up his wife and drove home, casually remarking, "Did I see you leaving with a friend?"

"Oh no," she replied, "she was just one of the delegates. What a tart! Flirted with anything in trousers and kept a few beds warm at night."

The husband was dismayed to hear this and was determined to find out from his mistress about his wife's behaviour. The next time he saw her, he casually asked about the conference and the sort of people that were there.

"I think I heard that one of the speakers came from my neck of the woods," he said.

"Oh yes," replied the mistress, "that would be Connie. She wasn't much fun. She came with her husband and they spent most of the time in their room!"

The efficiency expert concluded his lecture with a note of caution. "You don't want to try these techniques at home."

"Why not?" asked a listener from the back of the audience.

"I watched my wife's routine at breakfast for years," the expert explained. "She made lots of trips to the refrigerator, stove, table and cabinets, often carrying just a single item at a time. "Honey," I suggested, "Why don't you try carrying several things at once?"

The voice from the back asked, "Did it save her time?"

The expert replied, "Actually, yes. It used to take her 20 minutes to get breakfast ready. Now I do it in seven."

Arthur's wife nagged him relentlessly.

"It's just not good enough, Arthur. Every night you're down the pub and you never get back before midnight, leaving me here all alone time and time again. I've had just about enough!" she exclaimed.

So on this one particular night, Arthur took his wife along with him.

"What'll you have?" he asked.

"I'll have what you have," she replied.

A few minutes later, two pints of bitter were placed before them. Arthur took a sip, then his wife took a sip.

"Urrgh, this is awful!" she spluttered, "How the hell can you drink it?"

"You see!" replied Arthur triumphantly, "and you think I come out each night to enjoy myself."

A woman walked into a tattoo parlour and asked the tattooist if he would put a picture of a turkey on her left buttock and a picture of Father Christmas and a reindeer on her right buttock.

Now the tattooist was used to the strangest requests but this was so unusual he had to ask why.

"Well," replied the woman, "My husband's always complaining that there's never anything to eat between Thanksgiving and Christmas."

In her courting days, Jackie went out with a sailor and as a sign of her love she had his face tattooed on her left breast. But the passion went out of their relationship and they parted. The following year she met a soldier and had his face tattooed on her right breast but again, their love was short-lived.

Some years later, she met and married a pilot and one day as she emerged from the shower, he looked at her and laughed.

"What's that for?" she said angrily.

"I was just imagining the long faces on those two fellas in 10 years time!" he replied.

A newcomer to the neighbourhood was shocked and alarmed to see a couple acting outrageously in the field outside their house. The woman was tugging her tits up and down while the man was masturbating.

"Oh don't worry about them, they're deaf," said a voice behind him.

"She's telling him to milk the cow and he's telling her to go fuck herself."

COUPLING

Poor Doreen! She's had no luck. A few months ago a man asked if he could change her name to his. Of course she was delighted and said, yes.

Now he calls her Jimmy!

A man was desperate to meet someone of the opposite sex but he had low self-esteem because one of his eyes was made of wood. He got more and more despairing of the situation until his friends urged him to join a dating club. So he took the plunge and signed up. As luck would have it, a woman joined at the same time, and like him, she lacked confidence because she was very fat. Although both could see the other's shortcomings, they decided to meet and go for dinner. It was a great success. They found many shared interests and there was never an awkward moment.

"Would you like another glass of wine?" he asked.

"Oh yes, please," she replied.

"Would you like a coffee?" he asked later.

"Thank you," she replied happily.

As they left the restaurant, the man plucked up the courage to ask her for a kiss.

"Oh yes," she agreed.

As they kissed and cuddled, the man then asked the big question.

"Would you like to come back to my place?" he said nervously.

"Oh, wouldn't I!" she enthused.

"What!" he exclaimed angrily. "What gives you the right to call me wooden eye, you fat bitch?"

A widow of only a few months goes out on her first date since the death of her husband. They have a great evening but when he makes a move, she holds him back saying, "I can't. I'm wearing black knickers because I'm still in mourning for my husband."

They continue to date, although it never goes past a goodnight kiss at the end of the evening.

Then a few weeks later in the middle of a passionate embrace, he gets out a packet of black condoms.

"What are those for?" she asks.

"I'd like to give you my condolences!" he replies.

COUPLING

A man met a beautiful girl in the pub and couldn't believe his luck when she invited him back to her place. Very soon, they were upstairs, stripping off but just as he was about to throw himself at her she suddenly stopped and said,

"Oh, I should have told you, I went to the doctors today and he told me I had either VD or TB, but I can't remember which."

Even this news couldn't dampen the man's ardour. He rang up the girl's doctor straight away.

"I'm sorry," said the doctor. "I had two girls in today so I can't remember."

"Oh no!" exclaimed the man, "what shall I do?"

"Well chase her around the room a few times and if she starts to cough then go ahead and make love," came the reply.

Melvin was comforting his old friend.

"Don't worry," he said "I'll find a woman for your son to marry; bring him down to the club next week."

The following Saturday his friend's son arrived and was introduced to Moira. The boy turned away in disgust.

"Ugh, she's awful," he said. "She's got a face like the

back of a bus, a big moustache, one eye and very little hair."

"You don't have to whisper," said Melvin. "She's deaf as well."

The man pulled up outside his girlfriend's house and turned to give her a goodnight kiss. As he did so, he also pulled out his John Thomas and put it into her hand.

"How dare you!" she exclaimed, getting out of the car quickly. When she'd walked up the garden path to her front door, she turned and shouted angrily,

"I've only got two words to say to you, get lost!"

"Aarrgh!" he screamed back. "I've got two for you, LET GO."

The man parked the car in Lovers' Lane and for a few moments the young couple just sat and listened to the countryside noises.

"Oh it's lovely here," enthused the girl. "I think I can even hear the crickets."

"That's not a cricket," replied the man, "that's a zip."

COUPLING

The courting couple were looking for somewhere private but the gates of the park had been locked for the night.

"Never mind," said the boy, "if you stand on this (showing her his erect John Thomas) you'll be able to get over the wall."

"That may be so," she replied, "but how will I get back?"

A young couple were parked in Lovers Lane and after a bout of heavy petting, the boy whispered urgently.

"Go on Cath, let me put it in."

"Oh no", she replied, "We said we'd wait until we were married."

"Well just a little" he gasped "let me just put the head in to see what it's like."

She finally agreed but as soon as he began, he got carried away and thrust as far as he could go, in and out frantically.

"Oh George!" exclaimed the girl, "I can't wait, I can't wait, put it all in, please!"

George thought quickly and replied,

"Oh no Cath, we can't, remember our promise..."

The young man walked his girlfriend to her front door and started to kiss her.

"How about a quick blow job?" he said, "before I go."

"Oh no," she replied, "not here, anyone could pass and see us."

"Oh come on," he coaxed, "it won't take long, just a tiny little blow job."

"No, it wouldn't be right," she said adamantly.

For the next couple of minutes the man tried unsuccessfully to change her mind, then suddenly the front door was yanked open and a young girl stood there sleepy-eyed, obviously just having got out of bed.

"Dad says hurry up and give him a blow job, or he'll come down and do it, or I will, or someone will just as long as you take your bloody hand off the intercom."

The couple had been out on their first date and finished the evening back at her place in bed. As he struggled with her clothes, she said,

"You know I'm not that sort of girl really."

"I know," he replied, somewhat distracted. The girl burst into tears.

"What's wrong?" he asked looking alarmed.

"You… You're the first one," she sobbed.

"What? The first one to make love to you?"

"No, the first one to believe I'm not that kind of girl," she replied.

COURTROOMS

"Before I come to a decision on these divorce proceedings, does anyone wish to speak?" asked the judge.

The lawyer for the husband stood up and replied,

"M'lud, may I just bring to your attention once again, that what my client did was out of chivalry. Since when was it wrong to open a door for a lady?"

"I'm not disputing a chivalrous act," replied the judge, "but I think you're overlooking the fact that the car was travelling at 70 mph at the time."

The judge looked at the old woman and said, "Before I pass sentence, do you have anything to say in your defence?"

The old woman got to her feet and replied,

"Yes, Your Honour. The evening that it happened, I was sitting quietly on my porch when this beautiful young man came up to me and started to kiss my hand. Then he kissed my face and began rubbing himself up against me. He put his hands underneath my blouse and fondled my breasts. It was so wonderful, I opened my legs, Your Honour, and asked him to go all the way."

The old woman shook her head sadly as she remembered that evening. She continued, "That's when he laughed and said April Fool! So I picked up my rifle and shot him."

Just before the jury retired to contemplate the case, the judge summed up the evidence and finished by saying,

"Let us not forget that if someone's statement in court is different from their original interview with the police, this does not necessarily indicate a sign of dishonesty.

Why, even I have found myself in a similar situation. For instance, this morning I could have sworn that I was wearing my gold watch, but after some thought, realised I'd left it on the washstand in the bathroom."

The jury left the courtroom and were out all day, so the judge did not return home until late. When he walked through the door, he was surprised to see policemen all over the house.

"Oh Ronald, your gold watch has been stolen!" exclaimed his wife. "Nothing else, just the watch."

"My watch!" he exclaimed. "Now how would anyone know it was there!"

"I don't know," sobbed the wife. "It's just been one of those days. There's been any amount of people wanting to check the water pressure in the bathroom."

"Now madam," said the judge, "you are requesting a divorce on the grounds that your husband is a flat slob. What exactly do you mean?"

The woman thought for a moment and replied,

"Well, for instance, when we're in a café, he always drinks with his pinkie sticking out."

"Madam, there's nothing wrong with that. In some circles it's thought the height of good manners to drink tea with your little finger sticking out."

"Who said anything about his little finger?" she replied.

The judge looked over his glasses at the man standing before him.

"You are filing for divorce on the grounds of your wife's adultery. Is that so?"

"Yes, Your Honour."

"And do you have proof of this adultery? Can you name the man involved? Have you seen him?"

"Well, erm, no, not exactly, Your Honour. But I can tell you when I first knew about it," he added confidently. "It was one weekend 3 months ago. I had been away all week on a conference and didn't arrive home until late on Friday night. In the morning, we made mad passionate love when suddenly the woman in the flat next to us started banging on the wall and shouting, "Don't start all that again, for fuck's sake! Have you not had enough this week?"

"Will the defendant please rise," said the judge.

"Madam, you have been found guilty of killing your husband by pushing him off a 10-storey balcony. Before I pass sentence, is there anything you would like to say?"

"Yes, Your Honour," said the 84-year-old woman. "When I came home and found my husband in bed with another woman I guessed that if he could make love aged 96 years old, he could also fly."

"Do you have any questions?" the judge asked the learned counsel.

"Yes, M'lud. Mrs Smith, is it true that you committed adultery on the day of the 27 March, on the roof of the Dome, dressed in a baby doll outfit with a 60-year-old man wearing nothing but a necktie?"

Mrs Smith smiled and replied, "Can you repeat the date, please?"

Paddy was walking down by the canal when he saw a man throw himself in the water. Quick as a flash he jumped in after him and dragged the man to the side. But no sooner had he loosened his grip than the man plunged back in. Three times, Paddy dragged the man out and after the third time the man gasped, "Okay, okay, I won't go back in."

True enough, he didn't go back in. He ran to the nearest tree and hanged himself.

On the day of the inquest, the coroner remarked to Paddy, "I don't understand. You'd saved him three times from the canal, why didn't you cut him down from the tree?"

"Well, your honour, sir, I thought he was hanging himself up to dry," replied Paddy sadly.

"So, Mr. Smith, you want a divorce. On what grounds?" asked the judge.

"On the grounds that I live in a 2-storey house," he replied.

"I fail to see the significance of that," questioned the judge, "please explain."

"Well, Your Honour, one story is 'I've got a headache' and the second story is 'It's the wrong time of the month!"

DECEASED

Two women were taking tea at the Ritz and catching up on family news.

"I was so sorry to hear your Stanley had died," remarked the first woman. "I hope you've been able to carry on life without him."

"Yes, thank you," came the reply. "He was such a kind and thoughtful man. Do you know, hours before he died he gave me three envelopes which he told me would ease the burden once he'd gone."

"How thoughtful!" remarked the first woman. "What was in them?"

"Well, the first had £700 in it to buy a coffin. The second had £3,000 in it and a note saying 'Use this to give me a good send-off'. And let me tell you, they'll be talking about his funeral for years to come!"

"And what about the third envelope?"

"Oh, that said 'Use this cheque for £4,000 to buy a nice stone.' So I did," she said, holding out her finger to show a diamond ring, "what do you think of it?"

DECEASED

Mr and Mrs Green go out to see *My Fair Lady* on stage – the most sold-out show of the year.

Somehow, they've lucked into front row seats. But they notice that in the row behind them, there's an empty seat. When intermission comes and no one has sat in the seat, Mrs Green turns to the woman sitting next to it and asks, "Pardon me, but this is such a sold- out show, and in such demand. We were wondering why that seat is empty."

The woman says, "That's my late husband's seat."

Mrs. Green is horrified and apologizes for being so insensitive.

But a few minutes later, she turns around again.

"Without meaning to be rude or anything, this is an incredibly hard show to get into. Surely you must have a friend or a relative who would have wanted to come and see the show?"

The woman nods, but explains, "They're all at the funeral."

"I'm so sorry Bob, I hear you buried your wife last week."

"Had to," replied Bob, "She was dead."

Half way through the morning shift the manager of the warehouse noticed one of his men was crying.

"What's wrong Paddy?" he asked.

"It's my father," said Paddy. "I got a phone call this morning from Dublin to say he'd died."

"Oh that's terrible," replied the manager. "Why don't you take the rest of the day off."

"That's very kind of you, sir, but no thanks. It's easier to keep working."

A couple of hours later, the manager was concerned to see that Paddy was crying again.

"What's happened?" he asked.

"I've just had a phone call from my brother and his father has died as well," replied Paddy, wiping his eyes.

An old woman was seriously ill and decided she didn't want to live any longer. Hidden under the floorboards was a rifle that used to belong to her dear departed husband, so she decided to end it all and shoot herself in the heart. But not being too sure where her heart was, she rang up her best friend and asked her.

"It's about 2" under your left tit," came the reply, so she shot herself in the kneecap.

As the coffin was carried out of the church on the way to its final resting place, it was bumped against the wall and a moan was heard.

"Quick," someone said, "Charlie's still alive!"

And indeed, Charlie was not only alive but he lived for another 10 years.

On the occasion of his second funeral, as the coffin was once again being carried out of the church his wife said to the pallbearers,

"For goodness' sake, make sure you don't bump the wall again."

The youth turned to his friend and said,

"When it's time for me to go, I want to die in my sleep like Grandpa... not screaming and carrying on like the passengers on his bus."

What do you call a woman who knows where her husband is all the time?

A widow.

The doctor came out of the consulting room looking very serious.

"I'm sorry, Mrs Powers," he said, shaking his head, "but I'm afraid your husband is at death's door."

"Really!" she replied. "Is it possible to open the door and push him through?"

Two women talking over the garden wall.

"So what do you think, Beryl? Would it be fatal if your husband ran away with another woman?"

Beryl thought for a moment. "Yes, it could be. They say the shock of sudden intense happiness can be bad for the heart."

Following the death of her husband, a woman rang up the local newspaper to put a notice in the obituaries.

"Yes, madam," said the newspaperman, "what would you like to say?"

"John is dead," she replied.

Startled by the abrupt wording, he informed her, "Madam, you are allowed up to twelve words for the same price. Is there anything else you'd like to say?"

The woman thought for a moment and then replied, "John is dead. Set of brand-new golf clubs for sale."

"Jack, it's your brother, Bob, here," came the voice down the telephone line. "I'm not going to be able to get back for dad's funeral because I'm stuck in the Australian outback. Do something nice for him and send me the bill."

So Jack did as his brother wished and sent Bob a bill for £100 which Bob paid immediately.

However, the following month, Bob received another bill for £100 and this happened each and every month. Eventually he managed to catch up with Jack and asked him what was going on.

"Well, you said do something nice for dad," protested Jack, "so I hired him a nice black three-piece suit."

Why is it that only 15% of men go to heaven?

If they all went, it would be hell.

"You know, June, I've been thinking, I'd like to be cremated."

"OK John, I'll just go and get the car."

Bernard only had minutes to live as he beckoned his wife to come closer.

"Doris, please do one last thing for me, please ride in the same car as my mother on the day of my funeral. Then I can die a happy man."

The wife paused for a moment and then replied,

"Well, all right then, but you know it will completely spoil my whole day."

As the congregation left the church on Sunday morning, the vicar spotted Mrs Jessop.

"Good morning, good morning," he boomed, "and how's your husband?"

"He passed away last week, vicar," she replied.

"Oh, no, how did it happen?"

"He was in the allotment, digging up some potatoes for lunch, when he collapsed and died," she replied.

The vicar looked suitably sombre. "What on earth did you do?" he asked.

"Oh, not to worry, I had a packet of oven chips in the freezer."

June was dying. She only had a few seconds to live and she called for her husband to come a little closer.

"Fred," she whispered, "when I die I want you to marry Josie from across the street."

"Oh, no," replied her husband shocked, "I don't want to marry anyone after you."

"I insist," she gasped.

"But why?"

"Because I've hated that tart for more than 20 years."

No woman has ever shot her husband while he's been hoovering.

While his wife was still alive, the husband bought her a headstone engraved with the words "Here lies Doris, cold as usual."

The wife was so angry she immediately went out and got a headstone for him, with the words "In memory of Fred, stiff at last."

An old man was dying and his wife and family were standing around the bed. He had four tall and handsome blond sons and one small dark-haired boy. In the last few moments of life he beckoned to his wife and whispered,

"Patsy, my life is over, please tell me the truth. Is that small lad, that little one, is he mine?"

"Oh, yes, with my hand on my heart, I swear he is yours."

At that, the man died peacefully with a smile on his face.

"Phew," said the wife to herself, "thank goodness he didn't ask me about the other four."

DECEASED

An old man and a 20-year-old girl got married and for three weeks they were very happy, until one Sunday he collapsed and died.

Her mother arrived to console the unhappy girl.
"Oh, mum," she cried, "it was such a wonderful marriage. We were always so passionate, especially on Sunday when he would make love to the rhythm of the church bells."

The girl suddenly looked thoughtful. "Do you know, I'm sure he'd still be alive today if the fire engine hadn't gone past, clanging its bell so ferociously just minutes before he died."

Poor old Jake was lying on his death bed with the dutiful family sitting round, when he suddenly roused himself on smelling his wife's cooking in the kitchen. When she saw him open his eyes, she whispered gently to him, "Jake, my poor man, do you have a last wish?"

"Oh, Mary, that I do," he croaked. "May I just have a small piece of that wonderful cake you're cooking in the kitchen?"

"Oh, no," said his wife, "that's for after the funeral."

DECEASED

Bob and Harold had just arrived on the 10th fairway when a funeral procession passed by. Harold stopped playing, put down his golf club and took his hat off.

"That was a nice gesture," remarked Bob.

"Well, it was the least I could do, after all she's been a good wife to me over the past forty years."

Said the doctor to the old man,

"I'm sorry, Mr Hodges, you've only got three minutes to live."

"Oh, no!" exclaimed the man. "Is there anything you can do for me?"

"Well, I could get the nurse to boil you an egg."

An old shop keeper was dying and the family had gathered around his bed. All of a sudden, the old man raised himself up and said:

"Is Jean here?"

"Yes, I am," she replied.

"Is Robert here?"

"Yes, I'm here."

"And is Leonard here?"

"I'm here too."

"Then who the bloody hell is looking after the shop?" he cried.

There's nothing wrong with my husband that a good funeral wouldn't cure.

A long-suffering wife rang up the doctor's one evening and said urgently,

"Hello, doctor, my husband's lying at death's door. Could you possibly come and help him knock more loudly on it?"

The funeral procession made its way down the road, six close members of the family carrying the coffin between them. On top of the coffin was a fishing line, a net and some bait. A passerby remarked, "He must have been a very keen fisherman."

"Oh, he still is," came the reply. "He's off to the river as soon as they've buried his wife."

DENTIST

Bernard was really scared about going to the dentist but on this occasion he had no choice because of a raging toothache.

"Now come on, Bernard," coaxed the dentist, "we'll have it out in no time."

Alas, the man kept his mouth firmly closed. So the dentist took the nurse aside and whispered something into her ear. Moments later she firmly gasped Bernard's balls and gave them a sudden twist.

"Arrrgh!" screamed Bernard, and as he opened his mouth, the dentist quickly yanked out the offending tooth.

"There!" said the dentist, "that wasn't so bad, was it?"

"No, I suppose not," agreed Bernard, "but the fucking roots went down a long way."

DOCTOR, DOCTOR

"Doctor, doctor, tell me how I can live to be 100."

"Well, you'll have to be very careful in what you eat – no more rich food, only plain uncooked vegetables. And you'll have to give up alcohol and cigarettes. And sex of course is right out…"

"Then will I live to be 100?"

"No, but it'll soon stop you wanting to."

"Doctor, doctor, please help me," said the distressed woman. "I've got a zit on my face and growing from it is a spreading chestnut tree and a picnic table and chairs."

"Now don't worry," said the doctor soothingly, "it's only a beauty spot."

An old lady went to the doctors complaining of a bad stomach. After examining her, he suggested she keep a note of everything she passed and come back and see him the following evening. When she saw him the next day, she was feeling a lot better.

"That's good," he replied, "Did you pass anything unusual?"

"No, not really," she said, "one dog, two bushes and a line of washing."

"Good gracious!" he exclaimed, "no wonder you're feeling better!"

"Doctor, doctor, my hair is falling out," said the worried man. "Can you give me anything for it?"

So the doctor gave him a box.

After examining the woman closely, the doctor recommended a course of the male hormone, testosterone. Three months later, she returned to the surgery to let him know how she was getting on.

"I feel a lot better," she reported, "the only drawback is that I'm growing hair where I never used to have it."

"Don't worry," said the doctor "that's just a small side effect of the drug. Where are you growing the hair?"

"On my balls," she replied.

DOCTOR, DOCTOR

A man went to the doctor complaining of bad headaches.

"Instead of giving you drugs, I'm going to prescribe a completely different treatment," said the doctor. "It works because I've tried it myself. When I get a really bad headache I give my wife oral sex. As she reaches a climax, her legs squeeze my head tightly and it helps to release the tension. So you should do this every day for a month and then come back and see me."

"Thank you doctor, I certainly will," replied the man.

A month later, he returned to the surgery.

"Well, did it work?"

"Oh yes," replied the man. "I've never felt so good, it's a wonderful cure. By the way, your wife makes a lovely cup of tea as well."

The Lord of the Manor visited the doctor complaining of feeling unwell.

"Well, it could herpes or chicken pox," said the doctor. "We'll carry out a few tests and let you know the results tomorrow."

When Lord Farthing returned the next day he was told that the tests confirmed he had herpes.

"Well, I could have told you that," replied the Lord scornfully. "Where on earth would I get chicken pox from?"

"Doctor, doctor, there's something terribly wrong with me. Every part of my body hurts. If I touch my head it hurts, if I touch my leg it hurts, my body, my arm – everything I touch hurts."

"Ah, I see the problem," said the doctor, "you've broken your finger."

One night, a woman opened her front door to find a huge cricket on her porch. Before she had time to react, it gave her a violent push and then ran off. The following night, the cricket appeared again and kicked her hard on the shins. On the third night, it bit her on the hand. By this time, the woman was so distressed that she went to see her doctor.

"Ah, yes," said the doctor, "I've heard there's a nasty bug going around."

"Doctor, doctor, my young son has swallowed a razor blade."

"Now calm down, I'll be over straight away. Have you done anything?"

"Yes, I've shaved with an electric razor."

"Doctor, doctor, I'm really worried about my wife," said the distraught husband. "She's posing in the nude."

"Well, that's nothing to get too concerned about," the doctor replied. "It's just her expression of freedom."

"Yes, but this was for her passport picture!"

"Martin, why do you always close your eyes when you drink your beer?" asked the curious barman.

"Doctor's orders," he replied, "he told me never to look at a pint again!"

The woman was so overweight that her health was suffering but she was unable to keep to a strict diet. Eventually, the doctor gave her the news that she would no longer be taking any food through her mouth. From now on she would take all nourishment through the rectum. Two months later, she returned to the surgery with the good news that she had lost three stones.

"Well done," congratulated the doctor, "keep on like this and we'll soon have you down to a reasonable size."

The woman smiled happily and walked towards the door.

"Just one thing," said the doctor noticing she was walking with a strange waddle, "Is there anything wrong with your legs?"

"Oh no, doctor, they're fine."

"Then why are you walking in that strange way?"

"I'm only chewing some bubble gum, doctor," she replied.

"Doctor, doctor," says the worried man. "Something strange is happening to me. Every night when I go to bed, all I've got playing in my head is 'What's New Pussycat' and then when I wake up in the morning 'The Green Green Grass of Home' is going round and round in my brain. But that's not all. During the day I keep humming 'Delilah'. I think I must be going insane."

"No, you're not going insane," replies the doctor. "It's quite simple really. You've got Tom Jones Syndrome."

"Oh no!" despairs the man. "Is it a common complaint?"

"It's Not Unusual," replies the doctor.

A man went to the doctor's to find out if anything could be done for his baldness.

"Well, we could try some hair creams or a transplant," suggested the doctor, "but it's not 100 per cent guaranteed."

"No, no," said the man in despair. "I've tried creams already and I can't afford a transplant."

"Hmm," the doctor thought for a moment and then said: "Okay, I do have one other cure, but I warn you, it's a bit unusual."

"Oh anything, anything," pleaded the man.

"Okay. You need to put some female secretions on the bald patch."

"Thank you," said the man. "I'll give it a try, but I can't help noticing that you have quite a bald patch yourself."

"That's true," agreed the doctor "but have you also noticed my wonderful moustache?"

"Doctor, doctor, please help me," said the worried man, "I think there's something dreadfully wrong with me."

"And what are the symptoms?" asked the doctor.

"I can't stop frying things. Everything I eat, I fry first. Even puddings! I fry rice pudding, jelly, trifle, absolutely everything. But it now seems to be spreading to other things. I fry the newspaper before I read it. I fry my shoes and all my clothes. Why! I even fried my bicycle."

"Well, that's quite simple to diagnose," said the doctor. "You're frittering your life away!"

"Hmm, I see you've been circumcised," remarked the doctor.

"Oh no," replied the young man, "just wear and tear."

The woman had to confess that the grazes on her knees and elbows were due to having sex doggy fashion in the outside yard.

"My goodness!" exclaimed the doctor, "why on earth don't you do it in a more conventional way?"

"Well, there's a bit of a problem," she replied, "my dog's quite ugly, and his breath stinks."

As two doctors were taking lunch in the park, a man approached, shuffling along with his knees pressed together, fists clenched and doubled up.

"What do you reckon is wrong with him?" the first doctor asked his colleague.

"Severe arthritis, I would think. Do you agree?"

"No, I think its cerebral palsy," he replied.

All of a sudden the man came up to them and said through tight lips,

"Can you tell me where the Gents is, please?"

DOCTOR, DOCTOR

A man went to the doctor's with a broken leg.

"How did this happen?" asked the doctor.

"Well, it started fifteen years ago…" began the man.

"No, no," interrupted the doctor. "I want to know how you broke your leg now, today."

"But I'm trying to explain," said the man. "Fifteen years ago I used to work on a farm and every evening, the farmer's daughter would come over and ask me if there was anything I wanted. She was very persistent, said she'd do anything for me, but I was quite happy, I didn't need anything. Then this morning, when I was tiling the roof, I suddenly realised what she'd meant all those years back and the shock made me fall off the roof."

A man went to the doctors complaining of having no feeling in his buttocks. After a thorough external examination, the doctor asked him to bend over so he could examine his nether regions.

"Ah ha!" exclaimed the doctor, "there's some money stuck up your bum."

The doctor pulled out the cash and began to count it. "There's £1,999 here," he said.

"Well that explains it," replied the man. "I've not been feeling too grand!"

A man goes to the doctor complaining that his wife has lost all interest in him and she won't have sex. He pleads with the doctor for help so after a moment of deliberation the doctor gives him some tablets.

"Put one of these in her cocoa before going to bed," says the doctor, "but only one. Use one only, as they're very powerful."

So the man returns home and that night he drops a pill in his wife's cocoa. Then he drops a second one in for 'good luck'. But moments later, the doctor's orders come back to haunt him – 'only one' he hears the doctor say, so to ease his conscience he puts one in his own cocoa as well. A little while later, they retire to bed. The wife strips off and the pill begins to work.

"Ooh!" she says. "I need a man."

"Me too!" replies the husband.

A man went to the doctor and handed him a note, which said, "I've lost my voice, I cannot speak."

"We'll soon put that right," said the doctor. "Take your willy out and put it on the table here." The man did as he was instructed and the doctor whacked it as hard as he could with a baseball bat.

"Aaaah!" screamed the man in agony. "Good, good!" said the doctor. "Tomorrow we'll try B."

DOCTOR, DOCTOR

A voluptuous young woman walked into the doctor's with a baby in her arms.

"I'm worried about the baby," she told him "he doesn't seem to be gaining any weight."

"Hmm," mused the doctor, "is it breast fed or bottle fed?"

"Breast fed," she replied.

"In that case, I'd better examine you. Would you kindly strip to the waist."

The woman did as she was asked, revealing the most perfect pair of breasts. He fondled them in his hands and tweaked her nipples.

"Well that's the problem," he said, "you're not producing any milk."

"I know," she replied. "I'm the baby's aunt. But never mind, it was nice to meet you."

Dear Dr. Ruth,

I am sitting at my PC emailing to tell you my problem. It seems I have married a sex maniac. For the past 12 years he makes love to me regardless of what I am doing... I can be ironing, cooking, cleaning, sweeping, cleaning the cat box, or writing letters. He just comes right at me and won't be dissuaded for any reason. I would like to know if there is anything that ucnn hlp m wth f

unothel   gothsl ehj fpslth3/   o,,   fjsl; (o ------   .

lp sld mpskdlli

dlks, a;ld:;' . . . . .

DRUNK

The policeman said to the drunk on the street corner,

"Come on mate, time to go home, you've been standing here ages."

"Ah ha," replied the drunk. "I've heard the world goes round every 24 hours so I'm waiting for my house to appear... Oh look, it won't be long now, there's my next door neighbour."

Every night of the week, Jack would stagger home after the pubs closed and every night of the week his wife would be waiting on the doorstep, ranting and raving.

"Oh Doris," she confided in her friend, the next day. "I'm so fed up with this, it doesn't seem to matter what I say, he just goes on getting drunk."

"Well maybe you're reacting in the wrong way," replied Doris, "why don't you try being nice to him and see what happens?"

So the following evening Jack arrived back, drunk as usual, but this time his wife remained calm.

"Come and sit yourself down," she said, giving him a kiss, "and I'll make you a lovely hot cup of tea."

After he'd drunk it, she whispered seductively,

"Shall we go up to bed now?"

"Might as well," he replied. "I'll be in trouble anyway when I get home."

Two men had been drinking in the bar all afternoon and were sozzled.

"I'll never forget the day I turned to the bottle as a substitute for women," said one.

"Why?" asked the other.

"Because I got my dick stuck in it."

A drunk staggers out of a bar and makes his way over to the car park where he begins to rub the roof of every car. The car park attendant watches him in amazement and finally goes over to speak to him.

"Hey mate, why do you rub the roof of every vehicle?"

"I'm looking for my car," he slurs, "and I know it's got two blue lights and a siren on the top."

DRUNK

It was 11.30 at night when Jack finally got home from the pub, much the worse for wear.

"Oh Jack!" exclaimed his wife in dismay. "What a smell! Your head's covered in cow dung. Where have you been?"

"Sorry love," he said, burping. "Decided to cut across Farmer Giles' field on the way home and my cap flew off. I must have tried on half a dozen before I found the right one."

Two drunks were staggering along the pier when one tripped and fell into the sea.

"Help!" he cried, "help me please, I can't swim. Help, help, I can't swim!"

The other drunk replied, "Well neither can I, but I don't go around making such a bloody fuss about it."

DRUNK

A man was doing press-ups in the park when a drunk staggered past. Moments later the drunk returned, doubled over in laughter.

"What's so funny?" said the man gasping.

"I've got some bad news for you mate," grinned the drunk, "your girlfriend's gone home."

Every morning when the nurse came to change the old man's bed she would find shit all over the sheets. Finally, her patience snapped and she turned on him angrily.

"Right, that's it," she said, "if you do this once more, you can change your own sheets."

However, the next morning he woke up to find he'd done it again. He jumped out of bed, bundled up the sheets and threw them out of the window. As it happened, a drunk was staggering by at the time and the sheets landed on his head.

"Arrgh!" he screamed, punching wildly at the sheets until he finally wrestled free. He high-tailed it off to the nearest bar where he asked for a double scotch "and make it quick!" he gasped.

"Why, what's wrong?" asked the bartender.
"You'll never believe this," said the drunk, "but I've just beaten the crap out of a ghost."

DRUNK

A drunk staggers up to the bar and asks for a pint of beer. As he takes his first sip, he sees three darts on the table in front of him and asks the landlord why they are there.

"Well, sir, if any of my customers can get all 3 darts in the bull's eye, then they win a prize."

"That sounds good," slurs the drunk who immediately picks up the darts and starts to aim but he's so drunk, other customers in the bar have to point him in the right direction before he can even begin. However, much to everyone's astonishment, he gets all 3 darts in the bull's eye even though he's so unsteady on his feet that he twice falls to the ground.

"Bloody hell!" says the landlord, "no-one's managed that before, what the hell shall I give him?" He looks frantically around the room and his eyes rest on the old tortoise, which is in a box next to the fire.

"Here," he says, picking up the tortoise and giving it to the drunk, "this is your prize."

Smiling in delight, the drunk staggers out of the door and disappears.

The incident is soon forgotten and the pub carries on as normal, until 6 weeks later, the drunk reappears. Once again he staggers up to the bar and orders a pint. Suddenly, he sees the darts and remembering what happened before, he picks them up and throws them at the board. This time his hair is covering his eyes and his hands are shaking uncontrollably, yet he gets all three darts in the bull's eye.

"I don't fucking believe it!" exclaims the landlord, "how does he do it!"

"Okay, what do you want for a prize?" he asks.

"Same as last time," grins the drunk, "that beef in a crusty roll was great!"

A drunk staggered into a bar and asked for a drink.

"I'm sorry," replied the barman, "I think you've had enough. Go home and sleep it off."

The drunk left but came back a few minutes later and asked for a drink.

"No," said the barman firmly. "I'm not serving you."

Again the drunk left the bar only to reappear five minutes later.

"Look," said the barman impatiently, "I'm not serving you any more beer, you're too drunk."

"Okay," said the drunk, "I guess you must be right. That's what they said in the last two pubs as well."

"My problem is I love women too much," said the drunk sitting at the bar. "In fact it was a woman who drove me to drink and I feel really bad about it. I never wrote and said thank you."

"Now listen carefully," said the doctor to the drunk, hoping to scare him into doing something about his drinking. "If you carry on hitting the bottle, you'll begin to shrink and eventually turn into a mouse."

The drunk stumbled home, deep in thought. When he entered the house, he called to his wife, "Carol, do me a favour. If you see me getting smaller, for fuck's sake, get rid of the cat."

It was 2 o'clock in the morning and very cold when a couple were woken up by a loud knocking at the door.

"Go on John," nudged his wife, "you'd better find out who it is because it might be important."

Poor John had to get out of his nice warm bed and go downstairs. When he opened the door, he was confronted by a very drunk man who said, "Can you give me a push?"

"What!" exclaimed John, "how dare you disturb me at this time of the morning, now bugger off."

"Who was that?" asked his wife when he got back into bed.

"Some drunk idiot wanting me to give him a push," he replied. "I soon saw him off!"

"Oh John, how could you!" admonished his wife. "Don't you remember how we once broke down in the middle of nowhere and if it hadn't been for that kind man that stopped to help us, we'd still be there."

"Alright, alright," grumbled John, as he got out of bed a second time and went downstairs. He put on his coat, opened the front door and called out

"Hello, do you still want a push?"

"Yes please," came the reply.

"Where are you?" asked John.

"I'm over here."

John looked around, but couldn't see anyone. "Where are you exactly?" he called

"Over here!" shouted the drunk, "On the swing."

DRUNK

A drunk was staggering through the park scattering bits of paper as he went along.

"Excuse me, sir," said the park keeper, "you're throwing litter everywhere, what's going on?"

"Well, you see," said the drunk, looking furtively around, "I'm keeping the lions away?"

"Lions! But we don't have any lions here."

"No," smiled the drunk, "it works really well, doesn't it?"

A guy walks into a bar and says to the bartender, "I want you to give me 12-year scotch, and don't try to fool me because I can tell the difference."

The bartender is sceptical and decides to try to trick the man with 5-year scotch. The man takes a sip, scowls and says, "Bartender, this crap is 5-year scotch. I told you I want 12-year scotch." The bartender tries once more with 8-year scotch. The man takes a sip, grimaces and says, "Bartender, I don't want 8-year scotch like this filth. Give me 12-year scotch!"

Impressed, the bartender gets the 12-year scotch, the man takes a sip and sighs, "Ah, now that's the real thing."

A drunk has been watching all this with great interest.

He stumbles over and sets a glass down in front of the man and says, "Hey, I think that's really far out what you can do. Try this one."

The man takes a sip and immediately spits out the liquid and cries, "Yechhh! This stuff tastes like piss!"

"It is!" says the drunk. "Now how old am I?"

"Waiter!" called the woman, "I'm feeling a little tipsy, can you bring something to sober me up?"

"Certainly, madam," he replied. "I'll bring the bill."

A drunk was on his hands and knees under a lamp post one night, obviously searching for something on the ground. A kindly passer-by stopped to help him but after 10 minutes they'd failed to find his missing tooth.

"How did it happen?" asked the searcher.

"I tripped over the pavement at the bottom of this street and knocked my tooth out on the wall" said the drunk.

"So why are you looking for it here, if the accident happened at the bottom of the street?" asked the puzzled man.

"The light's better here," he replied.

DRUNK

A drunk staggered into the foyer of the cinema and bought a ticket for the film. He disappeared inside but returned a moment later and bought another ticket. Yet again he emerged some minutes later requesting a third ticket. The ticket seller looked extremely surprised and commented on his reappearance.

"This is the third ticket I've sold you in as many minutes. What's the matter?"

"It's like this," replied the drunk. "Every time I go through the door to find my seat, this big man comes up to me, snatches my ticket and tears it in two. And let me tell you, he's too big to argue with!"

"I demand another room immediately," said the drunk, staggering up to hotel reception.

"But I don't understand," replied the receptionist, puzzled, "all the rooms are exactly the same."

"I'm not going to argue," insisted the drunk. "Just change my room now."

"Of course, sir," said the receptionist. "I'll give you the key to room 85. But if you don't mind me asking, what's wrong with the room you have now?"

"It's on fire," he replied.

EDUCATION

The human biology course took place on a Monday afternoon and this week the subject was the male genitalia. The professor delighted in embarrassing his female students and began a story about a tribe of natives whose todgers were so long... At this point, one of the girls had had enough. She stood up and walked to the door only to have him remark loudly,

"You needn't be in such a hurry, my dear. The next plane for Africa doesn't leave until tomorrow."

The professor is discussing human reproduction with his students.

"Bob, once the baby is born can you name three advantages for using mother's milk?" he asks one of his students.

Bob replies,

"Well... it gives the baby better protection from germs, it's full of vitamins and minerals and erm..." but Bob couldn't think of a third reason.

The professor turns to the student next to him.

"Darren, can you think of a third advantage?"

"Yes sir," he replies, "it comes in such attractive packaging."

A college professor had just finished explaining an important research project to his class. He emphasized that this paper was an absolute requirement for passing his class, and that there would be only two acceptable excuses for being late. Those were a medically certifiable illness or a death in the student's immediate family.

A smart-alec student in the back of the classroom waved his hand and spoke up.

"But what about extreme sexual exhaustion, professor?"

As you would expect, the class exploded in laughter. When the students had finally settled down, the professor froze the young man with a glaring look.

"Well," he responded, "I guess you'll just have to learn to write with your other hand."

EDUCATION

"Good morning children," said the new teacher, "my name is Miss Prussy. Now if you find that difficult to remember, think of a pussy and just add an 'r'."

The following day, the teacher came into the classroom and said,

"Good morning children, I hope you've all remembered my name."

"Oh yes, miss," said a voice from the back, "it's Miss Crunt."

"Alice, you're late," said the teacher crossly.

"Sorry, miss, I had to walk to school today."

"Alright, just sit down and get your geography book out, we're looking at the British Isles. Now, can anyone tell me where the Scottish border is?"

"Yes Miss," said Alice. "He's in bed with my mum. That's why I had to walk to school today!"

The professor's voice boomed out across the lecture theatre,

"Today, we will study the human body in closer detail," he told his class of first-year medical students.

"Here in front of me is the dead body of a male aged 46. I shall remove parts of his anatomy. Here is the heart, here is the liver, these are the kidneys."

At that moment, a latecomer arrived and whispered to the student sitting next to him.

"Hey, what's he doing?"

"He's giving an organ recital," came the reply.

"Bobby," said the teacher, "can you give me another word for intercourse? Here's a clue. It's a four letter word ending in k."

Bobby jumped to his feet in anger.

"I know you don't like me, Miss," he said, "but you're not going to trick me into saying a bad word, just so that you can cane me!"

"Bobby, Bobby," she replied calmly. "I have no idea what you're talking about. The word 'talk' is not a bad word!"

EDUCATION

At the beginning of the English lesson, the teacher announced to the class that they all had to think of a sentence using the word 'marvellous'.

"Last night I went to the theatre and saw a marvellous show," said Bethany.

"I had a marvellous time on my holiday!" said Matthew.

Then Martin put his hand up. "Please miss, I've got a sentence. Last night my sister told my parents she was pregnant and my dad said 'Well that's marvellous, bloody marvellous'!"

The teacher addressed her class.

"Today, children, we're going to concentrate on English and I'm going to ask you all to think of a story which has a moral attached to it. What about you, Mary?"

"Well, miss. It was a very hot day and a little girl called Carol was walking along the river bank looking at the cool, clear water flowing by. As time went on, she felt so tired and sticky that she decided to go for a swim.

She ran behind a tree, changed into her swimming costume and without checking the riverbank she ran up to the edge and jumped in. Unfortunately, she'd jumped in just where a pile of rocks was jutting out of the water and badly grazed her legs. The moral of the story is 'look before you leap'."

"Not bad," commented the teacher. "Now you have a go, Peter."

"Bobby was a lazy boy and when he was told to collect the eggs from the hen house, he only took one small basket with him because he couldn't be bothered to look for another. Of course, the basket was soon filled but instead of making a second journey, he balanced the remaining eggs on top. Alas, on the way home, the handle broke and all the eggs fell to the ground and were smashed. So the moral of the story is 'don't put all your eggs in one basket'!"

"Well done, we'll just hear one more before the break. David, have you got a story?"

"Yes Miss. Uncle Harry was sent to France in the Second World War and on one occasion, he got left on his own. He ended up in a deserted village and while checking for enemies he found an old wine cellar. At that point, there wasn't much he could do so he drank a few bottles and stowed away a few more before carrying on. Then a short distance outside the village, he spotted a group of six Germans who had parked their tank at the side of the road. Quick as a flash, Uncle Harry killed three of them with a grenade and shot the rest with his machine gun. Then he smashed up the tank's controls so it couldn't be used again."

"And what's the moral of the story?" asked the teacher looking puzzled.

"Well miss, it's 'don't mess with Uncle Harry when he's pissed'."

The next day, the teacher continues her lesson on what the children's parents do for a living.

"My dad's a builder, miss," says Carol.

"That's good," replies the teacher, "your turn, Stephen."

"My mum's an airline stewardess," he replies proudly.

"Well, that's an exciting job, travelling all over the world."

The teacher looks around the classroom and notices Jake sitting very quietly in the back row.

"Come on Jake, tell everyone what your father does." "He's a cannibal, miss," says Jake hesitantly.

"I'm sorry Jake, I think I misheard. Can you repeat what you said?"

"He's a cannibal, miss."

"A cannibal! Whatever makes you think that?"

"Well, last night when I went past my parent's bedroom, I heard dad say, "Hurry up and turn the light off, and I'll eat you."

"Children," said the class teacher, "tomorrow we're going to learn about the facts of life so for tonight's homework I want you all to find out what a penis is."

Young Charlie returned home and asked his dad, who immediately pulled down his trousers and pointed proudly to his manhood.

"My son, that is a perfect penis."

The next day at school, Charlie's best friend came running up to him in a panic.

"I forgot to find out what a penis was, what shall I do?"

"No problem," said Charlie, "Look I'll show you."

They went behind a tree and Charlie pulled down his trousers.

"There," he said, "that's a penis and if it was a bit smaller, it would be a perfect penis."

EDUCATION

A man moved 500 miles across country to buy a secluded cottage and a small piece of land. Once he'd settled in and got the house in order, he decided to buy some animals for his smallholding. One morning he set off early to visit a neighbouring farm.

"I wonder if I might buy a rooster from you?" he asked the old farmer.

"Aye, that's alright," said the farmer, "but round here, we call them cocks."

"OK, thanks. May I also buy a chicken?"

"Here we are," said the farmer showing him a fine bird "but round here we call them pullets."

The man was just about to set off with his two birds when he noticed a donkey grazing nearby.

"Would you be willing to sell the donkey?" he asked.

"Certainly. You won't be disappointed with him. He's a good little worker but sometimes if he gets stubborn, you need to scratch him between the ears. Oh, by the way, round here we call them asses," said the farmer.

So off the man went with his new purchases but as they neared his cottage, the donkey suddenly stopped in his tracks and no amount of persuasion would make him move.

"Damn," cursed the man under his breath, but just then he noticed a smartly dressed woman walking by.

"Excuse me, madam," he called "would you hold my cock and pullet while I scratch my ass?"

The medical students were listening to a lecture on the importance of observation, given by Professor Hoodwink.

"It is very important to look at everything very carefully; to taste, to smell, to touch," he said.

Then he picked up a glass of urine.

"Look at this," he continued. "I see it's yellow, I smell it and I taste it."

The students gasped as he dipped his finger in the liquid and put it in his mouth.

"Now you try," he said.

The students were horrified but if he could do it, then so could they. In turn, each of them dripped their finger in the liquid and put it to their mouth.

"Now that is very interesting," said the professor. "We are talking about the importance of observation yet none of you noticed I dipped my second finger into the urine, but put my third finger into my mouth!"

The class teacher was asking the children what sort of jobs their parents had. One said his mother was a doctor, another said his father was an engineer. Young Martin said his mum was a whore. The teacher was outraged and sent Martin straight off to see the headmaster. Some time later, he returned and the teacher asked him what had happened.

"Please miss," said Martin, "the headmaster gave me an apple and asked for my phone number."

Wee Jimmy McDougall left his beloved Isles to go to a university in England. After he'd been there a couple of months, his family came to visit.

"So, bonny lad, how's it going?"

"Fine, fine," replied Jimmy, "though I've got some awful strange neighbours."

"Aye?"

"The one in the room on my right keeps banging his head against the wall all the time, and the one on the left keeps screaming."

"So how d'you cope with that?" they asked.

"Oh I take no notice," he replied. "I just keep on playing my bagpipes."

"Miss, miss," said the young boy. "I've just been circumcised and my willy's sore."

The teacher suggested he go ring his mother and tell her, so the boy did this and then returned to class.

Some time later, the teacher passed his desk and was shocked to see his willy hanging out of his trousers.

"What's going on?" she demanded.

The boy explained. "I told mum how I felt and she told me to stick it out till lunchtime and then she'd come and get me."

Tommy arrives home from school and sees his mum in the kitchen.

"What's this?" she asks, looking at the clock. "Why are you so early?"

"I was the only one to answer the teacher's question," he replies.

"Well done," she says, "and what was the question?"

"Who threw the rubber at me?"

FARMING

The farmer was sitting reading his weekly magazine when he said to his wife,

"Listen to this. It says here that it's only in humans where the female achieves an orgasm."

"Really!" she sneered, "prove it."

The farmer disappeared and arrived back an hour later.

"Well it doesn't happen in sheep and cows," he said, "but I couldn't be sure with pigs, they always make so much noise squealing."

An old farmer didn't often get the urge, but when he did, he had to act upon it immediately.

One day he was ploughing down in the bottom field, when he felt a mighty erection coming on.

"Bloody hell!" he shouted, running madly for the house and waving his arms frantically to get the wife's attention. He rushed through the door to find her scrubbing the kitchen floor.

"Quick, quick!" he panted, "get upstairs and strip off while I've still got the urge."

Sadly, by the time she did as he wished, the moment had passed and he was unable to perform.

"Now Martha!" he said forcefully, "don't hang around next time. When you see me rushing home, get upstairs immediately."

A few weeks passed and one afternoon, as the wife looked out of the window, she caught sight of her husband rushing towards the house waving frantically. Straight away she ran upstairs, stripped off and got into bed.

"Martha, Martha!" he called "where are you?"

"I'm up here," she replied, "waiting for you."

"Well get down here!" he yelled, "the bloody barn's on fire!"

"I have to go to market," said the farmer to his foreman "So I'll leave you in charge. Old Bernie Jenkins is coming over to see the bull, tell him its £100 a go if he wants his herd serviced and £200 if he wants the ram as well."

Later on in the morning, a car drew up outside and an angry man stormed across the farmyard.

"Where's Chivers!" he roared, "that bloody son of his has got my daughter pregnant."

"Well he's not here at the moment," replied the foreman, "and he didn't tell me how much he charges for that!"

The local radio station was doing a feature about life on isolated farms. They interviewed one such farmer and asked him whether it was true that people like him shagged cattle, sheep, goats and chickens.

"What!" roared the outraged farmer, "chickens!?!"

One morning, the farmer's wife woke up, looked out of the window and saw their only cow lying dead in the field.

"Oh no!" she wailed, "now we have no animals left, what can I do, how can I feed us?" and she was so distraught, she hanged herself.

When the farmer woke up, he discovered his dead wife and was so overcome with grief, he shot himself. So three sons were left on their own. The first son went walking along the seashore and met a mermaid.

"Don't look so sad," she said. "If you have sex with me five times, I will bring your family back to life and restore your farm to its former glory."

So the boy gladly took up the offer, but by the fourth time he was struggling and was unable to perform at all on the fifth attempt. Bitterly disappointed, he walked into the sea and drowned himself. Some time later, the second son came by and bumped into the mermaid.

"Do not despair," she said. "If you can make love to me ten times, I have the power to bring back your family and make the farm successful."

Eagerly the boy agreed and began with determination. Alas, he failed after number seven and was so ashamed he walked into the sea as well.

So there was only the youngest son left. He went looking for his brothers and was met by the mermaid. She told him what had happened but assured him that all could be put right if he made love to her twenty-five times. The boy thought for a moment and replied warily,

"Yeah, but how can I be sure it won't kill you like it did the cow?"

FATHERS

A little girl wandered into the bathroom while her father was taking a shower.

"Daddy, daddy, what's that?" she asked, pointing at his tackle.

"Well… erm… It's a hedgehog," he replied.

"Gosh!" she exclaimed, "it's got a hell of a big dick."

A keen country lad applied for a salesman's job at a city department store. In fact it was the biggest store in the world – you could get anything there. The boss asked him, "Have you ever been a salesman before?"

"Yes, I was a salesman in the country," said the lad. The boss liked the cut of his jib and said, "You can start tomorrow and I'll come and see you when we close up."

The day was long and arduous for the young man, but finally 5 o'clock came around. The boss duly fronted up and asked, "How many sales did you make today?" "One," said the young salesman.

"Only one?" blurted the boss, "most of my staff make 20 or 30 sales a day. How much was the sale worth?"

"Three hundred thousand dollars," said the young man.

"How did you manage that?" asked the flabbergasted boss.

"Well," said the salesman, "this man came in and I sold him a small fish hook, then a medium hook and finally a really large hook. Then I sold him a small fishing line, a medium one and a huge big one. I asked him where he was going fishing and he said down the coast.

I said he would probably need a boat, so I took him down to the boat department and sold him that twenty-foot schooner with the twin engines. Then he said his Volkswagen probably wouldn't be able to pull it, so I took him to the car department and sold him the new Deluxe Cruiser."

The boss took two steps back and asked in astonishment, "You sold all that to a guy who came in for a fish hook?"

"No," answered the salesman "He came in to buy a box of tampons for his wife and I said to him, 'Your weekend's shot, you may as well go fishing.'"

FLIRTING

A handsome but naive boy was discovered by police walking around town with just his shoes on.

"Hey, Malcolm, how come you're walking around naked?" they asked.

"Well it's like this," replied the boy. "I was on the river bank fishing when Mandy came along, sat down and started kissing me. Then she took all her clothes off and told me to do the same. So I did. I took all my clothes off except my shoes. Then she opened her legs and said, 'Go on Malcolm, go to town', so here I am."

A very shy guy goes into a bar and sees a beautiful woman sitting at the bar. After an hour of gathering up his courage he finally goes over to her and asks, tentatively, "Um, would you mind if I chatted with you for a while?"

She responds by yelling, at the top of her voice, "No, I will not sleep with you tonight!" Everyone in the bar is now staring at them.

Naturally, the guy is hopelessly and completely embarrassed and he slinks back to his table.

After a few minutes, the woman walks over to him and apologizes. She smiles at him and says, "I'm sorry if I embarrassed you. You see, I'm a graduate student in psychology and I'm studying how people respond to embarrassing situations."

To which he responds, at the top of his voice, "What do you mean $200?"

A woman was walking down the street when she stumbled, causing her glass eye to fly out. Fortunately, a man was coming the other way and he managed to catch it.

"Oh, thank you so much," she said. "Please let me treat you to lunch."

A few minutes later, they were seated in a bistro ordering food. As the waiter left, the man remarked, "Do you often treat men to lunch?"

"Oh no," she replied. "You just happened to catch my eye."

"Hello Sharon," greeted the arrogant man. "Tonight I'm going to buy you lots of drinks…"

"Oh no you're not!" she replied.

"Then I'm going to take you to dinner and buy you lots more drinks…

"Oh no you're not."

"And I'm going to take you clubbing…"

"Oh no you're not."

"And then back to my flat…"

"Oh no you're not."

"And I'm not going to wear a condom either."

"Oh yes, you are."

FRIENDS

Why did the Lone Ranger kill Tonto?

He found out what Kemo Sabe meant.

Two men talking in a pub.

"You know Don, every night my wife plasters her face in cold cream and puts curlers in her hair."

"Does it do any good?"

"No, not really. I can still tell it's her."

Three women were sitting around and bragging about their children. The first one says, "You know my son, he graduated first in his class from Stanford, he's now a doctor making $250,000 a year in Chicago."

The second woman says, "You know my son, he graduated first in his class from Harvard, he's now a lawyer making half a million dollars a year and he lives in Los Angeles."

The last woman says, "My son, he never went to any university but he now makes 1 million dollars a year in New York working as a sports repairman."

The other two women ask "What's a sports repairman?"

The woman replies, "He fixes hockey games, football games, baseball games....."

Three old women were sitting in the garden sipping tea and moaning about old age.

"It's getting to the point where I'll be in bed and I won't remember whether I'm going to sleep or just about to get up," remarked the first woman.

"Oh, I understand," said the second woman nodding her head. "My memory is so bad, sometimes I'll feed the cat ten times a day and at other times he doesn't get anything."

"Oh dear," sympathised the third woman, "thank goodness I don't get problems like that, touch wood," she said, knocking her hand on the table… "Oh! I'll just get the door."

FRIENDS

The Lone Ranger and Tonto were riding through a canyon when they heard the sound of many horses coming up behind them. Sure enough, 200 Navaho Indians in full war paint were bearing down on them. Suddenly, in front of them, came the sound of much yelling and 300 Apache Indians came riding into view.

The Lone Ranger turned to his trusted friend and said,

"Well Tonto, it looks like we're really in trouble this time."

Tonto replied, "What do you mean 'we', white man?"

Two women chatting over a cup of tea.

"Oh Flo, I was so depressed last week, I tried to kill myself by taking 500 pain killers."

"Oh no," gasped her friend. "What happened?"

"Well after two, I felt a lot better."

GAY TIMES

One prisoner said to the other,

"I think my cell mate's gay."

"How can you tell?"

"He closes his eyes when I kiss him goodnight."

A woman falls pregnant by another man and is so frightened of what her jealous husband might do, she pleads for help from her doctor. Now the doctor is quite sweet on the woman himself, so he agrees to help. When the baby is born, the doctor gives the newborn to a priest in the next ward who has just undergone an exploratory operation.

"I told the priest that a miracle had happened and he's the one who has given birth," the doctor tells the grateful woman. So the astonished priest is told the news of the miracle and devotes the next 16 years to bringing up his son as best as he can. But as each year passes, so the priest feels more and more guilt at what has happened. On the boy's 16th birthday, he breaks down and confesses all.

"I'm sorry son, I'm not your father."

"What do you mean?" demands the son.

"I'm afraid I'm your mother; your father is the bishop."

A convicted killer escaped from jail after 15 years and broke into a house to get provisions. He tied up the young couple as he went on the rampage from room to room.

"Karen," whispered her husband. "This doesn't look good. He'll stop at nothing to get what he wants so don't struggle. Just lay back and remember you may be saving our lives."

"Well, I'm glad you feel like that, darling," she replied, "He did mention what a cute arse you have."

Have you heard about the new lesbian sneakers called Alldykes?

Sales dropped dramatically when customers found the tongues weren't long enough.

An elderly man is put in an old people's home by his son.

"Don't worry dad, it's only on a trial basis and if you don't like it then we'll find somewhere else," he tells him, "and I'll ring every day to find out how it's going."

The following morning, the old man wakes up with a hard-on and the nurse who brings in his breakfast gives him a wonderful blow job.

"How's it going dad?" asks his son when he rings later in the day.

"Wonderful, wonderful," enthuses the old man "why this morning I had a hard on and a pretty nurse gave me a blow job. It was just perfect."

"Well that's good Dad, I'm glad everything's going well."

However, later in the day, as he's walking down the corridor, he drops his glasses and bending down to pick them up he gets molested. A male orderly whips out his todger and takes him from behind, giving him a right good seeing to. On the phone that night, he starts sobbing.

"Son, I can't stay here, it's a nightmare. I dropped my glasses today and got fucked up the backside by this huge male orderly. Come and get me please."

The son tries to calm him down.

"Now wait a minute, dad, don't forget about that pretty nurse. Isn't it worth staying there just for that?"

"No, no, you don't understand," says the old man in an anguished voice. "I only get a hard on once every two weeks, but I drop things at least half a dozen times a day!"

Two men get talking in a bar and after a couple of drinks one says to the other,

"Listen Karl, if you woke up in the morning with a sore arse, would you tell anyone about it?"

"No," replies Karl.

"How do you fancy going camping with me this weekend?"

GENIES

Monica Lewinsky was walking in the countryside when she spotted an old lamp in the undergrowth. It was covered in mud but as she began to rub the dirt off, a genie appeared in a puff of smoke.

"I am the genie of the lamp," it pronounced, "and I grant you one wish."

Monica thought for a few moments. She was famous and wealthy so what could she ask for? Then an idea came to her.

"I know," she said. "Could you make these love handles of mine disappear?"

"Of course!" replied the genie. And whoosh! Her ears fell off.

"Gerald, look at this," said his mate excitedly. "It's a magic pair of sandals. When you put them on, it makes you irresistible to women. Look, I'll show you."

His friend put on the sandals and sure enough, as he walked down the street he was continually mobbed by beautiful women.

"Bloody hell!" exclaimed Gerald, "let me have a go!"

Gerald put on the sandals and headed off down the

street but instead of being embraced by hoards of women, he found himself pursued by gay men at every turn.

"I don't understand," he said desperately. "What's happened?"

"You've got them on the wrong feet, you fool!" said his mate.

A man was walking along the beach when he discovered an old lamp that had been washed up onto the rocks. Picking it up, he was just in the process of rubbing off the dirt when a genie popped out of the spout.

"You have one wish," said the genie. "What do you want?"

The man thought for a moment and replied.

"I would like to be rich, dark and irresistible to women."

So the genie turned him into a box of Black Magic.

GENIES

A rabbit was being chased through the woods by a great macho grizzly bear when they bumped into a genie.

You have two wishes each," said the genie, once he had picked himself up.

So the bear said, "Well this is great! I would like to have such amazing sex appeal that it makes me irresistible... And... erm... for my second wish I would like all the other bears in the forest to be female."

"Shazam!" exclaimed the genie. "Your two wishes have been granted."

Then the genie looked at the rabbit.

"Ok, it's your turn," he said, "What would you like?"

Now the rabbit had been listening closely to the conversation between the bear and the genie, so he answered immediately.

"For my first wish I would like to get as far away from here as possible and secondly I wish for the bear to be gay!"

GOOD NEWS/BAD NEWS

The lawyer looked at his client and said,

"I've got good news and bad news. Your wife has found a picture worth £1 million."

"Well that's amazing!" exclaimed the client, "but what's the bad news?"

"It's a picture of you and your secretary."

HAGGLING

An isolated part of the country was being terrorised by a gang of ruthless bandits and people were fleeing their homes. In one village, all that remained was a young boy and his toothless, 85-year-old grandma.

One morning, they were woken by a tremendous noise as the gang rode into town.

"We want food," they demanded of the young boy.

"All I have left is one sausage and half a loaf of bread," he said.

"Then give it to us. War is war."

"Drink," they then shouted, "we want drink."

"There are only 3 bottles of beer left," replied the boy.

"Good. Let's have them now. War is war."

"Women. Bring us women," they yelled later.

"There is only my grandma," he said, pointing to the old hag who was smiling at them.

"Well… er… perhaps we'll forget about the women," one of them said, looking at the horrible sight.

"What do you mean?" said the old woman crossly. "War is war."

HEAVEN

Said God to the archangel, "I've just arranged for 12 hours of darkness to be followed by 12 hours of light – and this I'll alternate down on earth."

"So what are you going to do now?" asked the archangel.

"Oh, I think I'll call it a day," came the reply.

Three married couples arrived at the Pearly Gates at the same time and were met by St. Peter.

He said to the first couple, "May I have your names please?"

"Yes, of course," replied the husband. "I'm Bob Crossley and this is my wife Sherry."

"Oh I'm sorry," said St. Peter, "I can't let you in. I can't have anyone in here with a name related to drinking."

So the first couple walked away sadly.

St. Peter turned to the second couple. "Names please."

"I'm Martin Parker and this is my wife Penny."

"Oh dear," St. Peter said shaking his head. "No one can come in here if their name is related to money."

So the second couple departed.

Then before St. Peter could ask the third couple any questions, the husband took his wife by the arm and led her away.

"Come on Fanny, let's go," he said.

A nun dies and finds herself standing outside the Pearly Gates.

St. Peter says, "I know you have led a truly unblemished life, Sister, but I must ask you one question before you come in. What did Eve first say to Adam?"

"Gosh, that's a hard one," she replies.

"Well done," says St. Peter and opens the gates.

It's a nice day so Jesus and St. Paul decide to have a round of golf. They reach the 10th fairway and Jesus asks St. Paul for his advice.

"What should I use for this shot?"

"I'd use a 5 iron," St. Paul replies.

Jesus thinks for a moment. "I don't know," he replies, "I think Jack Nicklaus would use a 6 iron."

"No, no," said St. Paul "You've got to make sure you get over the lake and miss the bunkers on the right."

"No, I'm going with a 6 iron."

Jesus takes his shot and the ball plunges straight into the lake.

"Never mind," he says, and with that he walks across the water to retrieve the ball. Just at that moment, another golfer walks by and sees Jesus walking on the water.

He turns to St. Paul and says:

"Who does he think he is? Jesus Christ?"

"Oh no," replies St. Paul, "he thinks he's Jack Nicklaus."

Two men arrive at the Pearly Gates and as St. Peter signs them in, he shakes his head in disappointment.

"Oh dear, oh dear," he sighs. "I see from your records that both of you cheated on paying taxes back on earth, I'm afraid you'll have to pay a penalty for that."

So the two men enter heaven but are paired up with a couple of old hags who will be with them for eternity. Some months later, they bump into an old friend of theirs. On his arm is the most beautiful woman they've ever seen. The two men take him aside. "Wow! Bert, you've done alright for yourself," they say.

"Oh yes," he enthused. "Isn't she gorgeous? You want to see her in bed – talk about heaven! What puzzles me, though, is after we've made love, she always turns over and mutters, 'Bloody income tax'."

When Einstein died and arrived at the gates of heaven, St. Peter wouldn't let him in until he proved his identity.

Einstein scribbled out a couple of his equations, and was admitted into paradise.

And when Picasso died, St. Peter asked, "How do I know you're Picasso?"

Picasso sketched out a couple of his masterpieces. St. Peter was convinced and let him in.

When George W. Bush died, he went to heaven and met the man at the gates. "How can you prove to me you're George W. Bush?" Saint Peter said.

Bush replied, "Well heck, I don't know."

St. Peter says, "Well, Albert Einstein showed me his equations and Picasso drew his famous pictures. What can you do to prove you're George W. Bush?"

Bush replies, "Who are Albert Einstein and Picasso?"

St. Peter says, "C'mon on in, George."

HONEYMOONS

The newly married couple arranged to spend the night at the bride's parent's house before setting off on their honeymoon the following day. However, when they hadn't put in an appearance two hours before leaving for the airport, the bride's mother began to get worried.

"Has anyone seen June and Malcolm since yesterday?" she asked the rest of the family.

"I did," said the young son of 7. "Last night when I went to the bathroom, Malcolm asked me if I had any Vaseline. I wasn't sure what that was, so I gave him some of my modelling glue instead."

The honeymooners arrive at the 4-star hotel, covered in confetti.

"Aha!" said the receptionist, "you'll be wanting the bridal."

"Oh no," blushed the new bride, "I'll just hang onto his ears until I get used to it."

HONEYMOONS

Three daughters all got married on the same day and spent their honeymoon night in their parent's palatial mansion. The couples retired to bed early and some time later, the parents turned off the lights and went upstairs as well. Now the parent's bedroom was in the west wing and to get there, they had to pass their daughters' rooms. As they walked past the first door, they heard their daughter laughing. Behind the second door, they heard their daughter crying, but behind the third door there was no sound at all. The following morning, the parents took their daughters aside and questioned them about the night before.

The first daughter said, "Well, you always told me it was polite to laugh if someone told you a joke."

And the second daughter said, "You always told me to cry if I was hurt."

Finally, the third daughter said, "And you told me never to speak with my mouth full."

A man married a Japanese woman who had been brought up to please her husband as much as she could. On their honeymoon night, they spent many hours making mad passionate love and in the morning, when the woman got out of bed, she farted.

"OK 'scuse me," she said, "front hole so happy, back hole whistle."

HONEYMOONS

The vicar and his new wife were preparing for bed on the honeymoon night. But first the vicar said, "My darling, let's kneel down and pray together for strength and guidance."

She replied "Just pray for strength, Maurice, I'll do the guiding."

On the morning of the wedding, the bride-to-be asked her friend to buy a black sexy negligee and pack it in her going-away bag.

"I don't have time to do it myself," she explained, "and I do so want to look my best for tonight."

So the friend popped down to the shops but couldn't find a black sexy negligee anywhere. In the end she chose a short pink one and stuffed it quickly in the top of the bag. So the wedding took place and after much celebration the newlyweds left for their hide-away hotel. They retired to the bedroom and it was then that the bridegroom had last-minute nerves.

"Look Tracy," he said blushing madly, "I'm a bit shy, would you mind leaving me while I take my clothes off."

"Of course not, darling," she replied. "I'll change in the bathroom."

HONEYMOONS

So the bride took her bag into the bathroom, opened it and discovered the negligee.

"Oh no!" she said aloud, "it's short, pink and wrinkled."

"Hey!" came a voice from the other room. "You promised you wouldn't peek!"

HOSPITALS

A man had been so badly injured that he could only be fed rectally through a tube. When his wife arrived at the hospital to find out how he was, the nurse replied, "Oh much better, we're really pleased with his progress. It was good to see his arse snap at a bowl of cornflakes this morning."

As the man wakes up from a routine operation to have his tonsils removed, he sees a group of doctors standing around the bed.

"What's wrong?" he asks nervously, looking at their solemn faces.

"I'm afraid there's been a mix-up in taking your tonsils out; we've given you a sex change operation instead. We've taken away your penis and given you a vagina."

"Oh no!" wails the man, "this is dreadful. It means I'll never experience another erection."

"Now hold on a minute," replies the surgeon, "that's not necessarily true. You can experience another erection. It just won't be yours."

A man went into hospital to have an appendectomy but unfortunately the surgeon sneezed half way through and his knife slipped and cut off one of the man's testicles. In a panic, the surgeon replaced it with an onion. A few weeks later, the man returned for a check up.

"How's it going?" asked the surgeon.

"Oh fine," said the man, "apart from some odd side effects."

"Really!" said the surgeon with a sinking heart, "and what are those?"

"Well, every time I go for a piss, my eyes water. When my wife gives me a blow job, she gets indigestion and when I smell hamburgers, I get an erection."

The rugby player was rushed to hospital with a dislocated shoulder. As the doctor manoeuvred it back into place, he groaned and yelled out in pain.

"Stop acting like a baby," remarked the doctor, "a big rugby player like yourself should show a bit more courage. Now there's a woman next door who's having a baby and she's not making a fuss like you."

"Maybe not," replied the rugby player through gritted teeth, "but then in her case no one's trying to push anything back in."

A Scotsman, an Englishman and an Indian are pacing the waiting room of the local maternity hospital. All three are expecting their first babies and the tension is mounting. As luck would have it, all the babies are born within a few minutes of each other and the nurse appears some time later with some disturbing news.

"We've got the babies mixed up," she says, "so we hope you might be able to identify the one that is yours."

The Scotsman is first through the door and into the nursery.

"I'll have that one," he says quickly.

"Hold on," says the Englishman, "that's the brown baby, you must know that can't be yours."

"I know," replies the Scotsman, "but this way I know I haven't picked the English one!"

A pretty nurse went along to the psychiatrist.

"I've got an awful problem," she said, "every new doctor I meet, I end up in bed with him. But afterwards I feel so guilty and depressed."

"So you want me to stop your urges to jump into bed with all these doctors?" asked the psychiatrist.

"Well, no," she replied, "I want you to stop me feeling so guilty and depressed."

A man and a woman are sitting in a hospital corridor waiting to be called. They strike up a conversation.

"I'm here to give blood," she says, "it's £5 a pint, what about you?"

"I'm here to donate sperm" he answers, "its £30 each time."

"Oh really," she says, looking thoughtful. Some weeks later, the same two people meet again at the hospital.

"Have you come to give some more blood?" asks the man.

"Uh uh," she says, shaking her head and keeping her mouth closed.

HUNTING

Two men thought up a great idea for hunting down a rogue grizzly bear who had been terrorising the local neighbourhood. They dressed up in a female bear costume hoping to lure the grizzly close enough to shoot him. All went according to plan and in the middle of a forest clearing they heard the mighty roar of the bear as it strode into view.

"Quick, Fred," whispered the man at the front of the costume, "let's get out and shoot him."

"We can't," came the muffled voice at the back, "the zip's stuck. What shall we do?"

"Well I'm going to start stripping bark," said the voice at the front, "but you'd better brace yourself."

HUSBANDS

A man walked up to an attractive girl and said,

"I've lost my wife, do you mind if I talk to you."

"Why?" she asked.

"Because every time I talk to a pretty girl, my wife always appears out of the blue!"

"I demand to see the burglar who broke into our house last night," demanded the irate man to the duty officer.

"Now, now, sir," came the reply. "You'll have to wait until he appears in court later this morning."

"But I only want to ask him one question," said the man. "I want to know how he managed to get into the house without waking my wife up… I've been trying for years and I've never managed it."

The lights of the patrol car picked out a man staggering along the street at 2.30 in the morning. They pulled up beside him and one of the officers got out.

"Where are you going?" he asked.

"A lecture" replied the man.

"What! At this time of night? Who's giving it?"

"My wife," he replied.

"Doctor, I have a problem, I can't get sexually aroused for my wife," said the distraught husband.

"Now don't worry too much," replied the doctor, "just bring your wife in tomorrow and I'll see what can be done."

The following day, the man's wife came to the surgery with him.

"Hello, Mrs Plainly, would you mind taking all your clothes off and sitting on the bed with your legs in the air… That's fine, thank you. Now you can get dressed."

The doctor took the man aside and said confidentially to him. "Don't worry, it's not your fault. Your wife does nothing for me either."

HUSBANDS

"Hello darling," said the man to his wife as she walked into the pub. "What can I get you to drink, sweetheart?"

The order was given and the man went up to the bar. "You old romantic!" remarked the barman. "You always call your wife by such lovely names."

"Well, to be honest," replied the husband, "I forgot her real name about five years ago!"

INFIDELITY

A woman discovered her husband had been cheating on her, so the next time he went off to the oil rig she plotted her revenge. One morning a parcel arrived for the husband, containing a batch of home-made cookies and a video of his favourite TV programmes.

"Oh great!" he said, and invited his friends to come round and watch it with him that night after their shift had finished. They settled down, watched the video and munched away at the cookies. However, an hour and a half into the recording, it suddenly went blank and then a picture of his wife appeared giving his next-door neighbour a blow job. As he watched in horror, she spat the contents of her mouth into the cookie mixture, turned to the camera and hissed, "I want a divorce!"

Late at night, there was a knock at the door and when the wife answered, a man demanded, "Do you know how to have sex?"

The woman closed the door in alarm and the man went away. But for the next three nights he returned, shouting at her through the letterbox. "Do you know how to have sex?" he kept repeating.

INFIDELITY

Now her husband had been away on business for the week, but when he returned on Friday he could see she was very upset. It didn't take long for him to find out what had been happening so he advised her to open the door and he'd be waiting behind it to deal with the pest.

Sure enough, later that night, the man returned banging on the door. The wife opened it as he shouted, "Do you know how to have sex?"

"Yes, I do," she replied.

"Then give it to your husband," he said angrily, "and tell him to leave my wife alone."

After a good romp in the back seat, the man turned to his date and said,

"Do you tell your mother everything?"

"Oh, she's not interested," came the reply. "It's my bloody husband who's so nosy."

Instead of going home after work, the man took his secretary for a drink, then dinner, then back to her place for a session of wild sex. A few hours later, he realised he ought to be getting home so he dressed quickly, combed his hair and looked aghast at the love bite on his neck. How was he going to talk his way out of this one!

Later, as he opened the front door, the dog bounded up and greeted him wildly. Immediately the man had a great idea. He fell to the floor and allowed the dog to jump on top of him, just as his wife appeared in the hall.

"Look at this!" he said feigning anger. "Look what the dog's done to my neck."

"Well, that's nothing," she replied, opening up her blouse. "Look what he did to my tits."

The couple's marriage was on the rocks so the wife decided to go and see a psychiatrist. After 30 minutes of general chat, the subject turned to sex and it soon became apparent that the problem lay in this area.

"When you make love, do you ever watch your husband's face?" asked the psychiatrist.

"Well, I did once," she replied.

"Once!" he exclaimed, "and how did he look?"

"Very angry," she replied.

"Well, this is most extraordinary," he remarked. "Not only is it very unusual to have only seen your husband's face once, but I'm amazed to hear that he looked so angry. Can you give me some idea of what was happening at the time?"

"Yes, he was watching me through the kitchen window!"

A man was walking through Piccadilly Circus on his way home when he passed a novelty stand and there on the counter were lots of funny certificates. One said,

"The holder of this certificate is authorised to have 3 hours of sex every day, wherever she likes."

The man thought this was a great joke and bought it to take home to his wife as a silly present.

"I'm home darling!" he called as he went into the house, "and I've bought you a present."

The wife appeared from the kitchen, read the certificate and smiled broadly.

"Oh John, that's wonderful," she said, grabbing her coat. "Dinner's in the oven, I'll see you in 3 hours."

"Eileen, there's something I must ask you," said her husband. "Now that our five children have all grown up and left home, there's something that's always bothered me. It's Charlie. He doesn't look anything like the other four. Has he got a different father? Come on Eileen, just tell me. It's all in the past so I won't get angry."

The wife looked sadly at her husband and nodded her head.

"Yes Jack. You're right, Charlie does have a different father from the other four."

"I knew it," muttered Jack, sitting down in the chair. "Who is the father, Eileen?" he asked apprehensively. She looked at him cautiously and replied,

"You are, Jack."

"Darling, we've been married nearly 60 years and I'm still very happy. But in all that time have you ever been unfaithful?" he asked.

His wife looked at him in surprise.

"Well, if you must know, I was unfaithful just three times."

"Really! When?"

"The first time was when you put in for promotion to become the youngest general manager in the company and it all depended on the vote of Malcolm Havelot."

"So being unfaithful that one time has helped me work my way up to being one of the most successful men in our industry. Thank you, darling. When was the second time?"

"That was fifteen years ago when there was a threat of a by-pass being built at the bottom of our land. If you remember, there were two options and the final decision rested with the Planning Officer and the Environmental Surveyor."

"So you saved our house, how wonderful," he said in gratitude. "Even if you did sleep with two men at the same time. And the third time?"

"Okay, yes. You remember that time you wanted to restructure the company and you were 84 votes short…"

After spending two months abroad on business, a man came home to the loving embrace of his wife and son. They spent a delightful evening together, catching up on all the gossip and it wasn't until the next morning, that he noticed his son playing on an expensive games console.

"Where did you get that from son?" he asked.

"From hiking," replied the son.

"Hiking! Come off it," said dad, "you don't get money hiking. Now where did it come from?"

"Honest dad, it's true. While you were away, Mr. Miles from the council would come round to see Mum, and he'd always say to me, "Here lad, have this £10 and take a hike.""

A man came home from the pub earlier than usual to discover his best friend was in bed with his wife.

"Oh Jack!" he exclaimed, sadly shaking his head, "I have to. But you?"

Five minutes after leaving the house for work, the man realises he's forgotten some important papers. He turns round, gets home and walks into the kitchen to see his wife standing over the sink. Quick as lightning he goes up to her and grabs her tits from behind saying jokingly, "Now, what can I do you for today?"

"Just six eggs and a pint of cream please," she replies.

INFIDELITY

A man came home early from work to find his wife in bed with another man.

"What the hell are you doing?" he screamed.

"I'm listening to the music," said the stranger who had his head between the wife's breasts.

"Get off," said the husband, "let me have a go… Well I can't hear anything."

"Of course you can't," replied the stranger. "You're not plugged in."

Instead of going home, the man took his new young secretary out to dinner where they drank a lot and then went back to her place for coffee and bed. Alas, no matter how much he tried, he could not get an erection so eventually he went home, very embarrassed. He slid very quietly into bed, next to his fat snoring wife and as their bodies touched he finally got the erection he'd been trying for all night. Cursing under his breath, he got out of bed again looked down at his wondrous organ and said,

"No one wonder they call you a fucking plonker!"

INFIDELITY

Two men were talking over their pints of beer.

"You know Jack, yesterday I was reading in the paper that the world has too many people. We're running out of space."

"So?"

"Well it's true. When I went home last night, I found a man in our wardrobe."

A distraught wife raged at her husband.

"A mistress? You have a mistress, but why? What's she got that I haven't?"

So the husband told her.

"She's so wonderful in bed, she moans and groans all the time. Not like you, you're so unresponsive."

The following evening, the wife decided to show her husband just how good she could be. She turned to him in bed, roused his manhood and when he started making love to her, she began.

"Well, what a day I've had. First the car ran out of petrol and I had to walk 2 miles to the nearest garage, then it started to rain, our daughter was sick all over the carpet, the cat peed all over the kitchen floor…"

INSECTS

Professor Blenkinsop had made the study of spiders his life work. Now, after fifty years, he was revealing to the world, the results of his painstaking research.

He placed a spider on the table and told it to walk ten paces forward. The spider did exactly that. Then he told the spider to walk ten paces backwards and again the spider obeyed. The gasps of astonishment and applause from the audience were tumultuous.

Professor Blenkinsop put his hands up to quieten the crowd. Then he picked up the spider and pulled off all its legs.

"Walk ten paces forward," he commanded the spider. But it didn't move.

"Okay," he said, "walk ten paces backwards."

But still it didn't move.

The Professor turned to the audience and in his most solemn voice he declared,

"Ladies and gentlemen I have just proved without a doubt that if you pull the legs off a spider, it can no longer hear."

"Daddy, daddy," said the little girl, "what are those two insects doing?"

"Well my darling, they're doing what comes naturally. I've told you about the birds and the bees."

"And daddy, what are those two insects called?" she continued.

"Daddy long-legs."

"But daddy, one must be a mummy long-legs," she persisted.

"No, my little sugar plum, they're both daddy long-legs."

"Ugh!" she squealed, went up to the insects and squashed them underfoot.

"What did you do that for?" asked daddy, surprised.

"Well I'm not having anything like that going on in our garden!" she replied angrily.

"Three double whiskeys," said the flea, hopping up to the bar. He drank them one after another and then went rushing out of the door, jumped high into the air and landed with a crash on the ground.

"Bugger!" he cursed, "someone's gone off with my dog!"

JEWISH

A Jewish man stared sadly into his pint of beer and his sad demeanour attracted the attention of the barman. "What's up?" he asked.

The man sighed deeply and said,

"Three weeks ago my father died and left me £250,000 in his will."

"I'm sorry to hear that," said the barman. "It's always hard to lose a parent."

"And then two weeks ago," continued the man, "my wife died and her million pound estate came to me."

"Why that's awful!" exclaimed the barman. "Your poor wife."

"And only last week, my great aunt died leaving me £100,000."

"God Almighty!" said the astonished barman. "Three deaths in three weeks. No wonder you're looking miserable."

"So what happens this week?" said the Jewish man, holding out his hands and shaking his head, "Nothing, absolutely nothing."

A Jewish man is reading his newspaper when suddenly he exclaims loudly,

"Lynn, Lynn vot is syphilis, it says you can die from it, but vot is it? Many people get de syphilis."

"Now, now," says his wife. "I'll look it up in the medical encyclopaedia, don't panic."

Moments later, the wife returns with the book and smiles at him.

"Nothing to worry about old man, it says it only affects de gentiles."

A Jewish girl goes away on holiday and on returning, rings her mother from the airport.

"Hi mum, I've got some wonderful news. I met this gorgeous bloke and it was love at first sight. We've got engaged and I'm bringing him home to meet you. One thing though, he's not Jewish."

"Well, okay," replies Mum, "but I expect he's got a good job?"

"No he hasn't. He's unemployed. He doesn't want a nine to five job. He hopes to play in a rock band."

"Well, okay. Where will you live once you are married?"

"If it's alright, mum, we'd like to stay with you until we save up some money."

"Well, okay. Your dad can sleep downstairs and you can have our room."

"But what about you, mum? Where will you sleep."

"Me! Don't worry about me. As soon as you put the phone down, I'm going to drop dead!"

Two children were playing on the beach with their dog when a freak wave carried the poor animal out to sea. Luckily, a passing rabbi saw the plight of the dog so he dived in and dragged it from the water, laid it on the sand and gave it mouth-to-mouth resuscitation.

"Are you a vet?" asked the children.

"Am I a vet?" replied the rabbi. "I'm soaking."

JEWISH

Two Jewish businessmen travel up to London every day on the 8.15 to Waterloo. Then one morning Morrie turns to his companion and says,

"You know, it's amazing; after all these years of travelling together you never asked me how my business is doing."

"I'm sorry," replies his companion, "how is business?"

"Oh," says Morrie, "don't ask."

KIDS

A little boy wakes up in the middle of the night needing to have a pee. On the way back from the toilet, he hears a noise from his parent's bedroom, he peeks round the door and sees them in the throes of lovemaking.

Quietly, the boy creeps back to his own bedroom and wakes up his young sister.

"Come with me," he whispers and takes her along to see their parents.

"Look at that," he says, "and we get smacked just for sucking our thumbs!"

Late one night, the doctor was called out to the house of a woman expecting a baby. Unfortunately, the weather was very stormy and by the time he got there, the electricity had failed. He realised he would have to deliver the baby by candlelight so he was forced to ask for the help of the woman's young 5 year-old son.

Thirty minutes later, the baby was born and all was well, thanks in part to the young boy holding the candle. The doctor examined the new arrival and gave it a tap on the bottom to make it cry. At that point, the young son said forcefully,

"I'd smack him harder than that, he shouldn't have been up there in the first place."

"Mummy, Mummy, can I go and watch the builders next door please?" said the young six-year-old boy.

"Alright," replied mum, just don't get in their way."

So the little boy spent all day watching the workmen and when he came back for tea, Mum asked him if he'd enjoyed his day.

"Oh yes," he said enthusiastically, "it was great."

"Well, tell me about it," she said.

"I watched the plumber. He put the fucking pipe under the sink but the frigging seal was broken so he had to start the bloody thing again. It was a right bastard."

"Tommy!" gasped his shocked mother. "Wait till you father gets home, I'll let him deal with you."

So when Dad arrived home, he listened to what his son had to say and was so angry, he shouted loudly,

"Tommy, you need to be taught a lesson. Go out and get me a switch."

But Tommy replied,

"Go fuck yourself, that's the electrician's job."

"Sophie, what are you doing with my toothbrush?" asked Dad.

"I'm cleaning the dog's teeth," she replied. "But don't worry, I'll put it back when I've finished, like I always do."

As a little girl climbed onto Santa's lap, Santa asked the usual, "And what would you like for Christmas?"

The child stared at him open-mouthed and horrified for a minute, then gasped: "Didn't you get my email?"

"Tomorrow we will discuss human reproduction so I'd like you to go home tonight and find out as much as you can about the subject," said the class teacher.

Young Tommy went home and found his mother in the kitchen.

"Mummy, where did I come from?" he asked. Too busy to sit down and tell him the truth, she replied,

"A stork brought you, darling, and put you under the rose bush."

Tommy went into the dining room where his grandma was watching TV.

"Where did my mum come from?" he asked her.

Now Grandma didn't discuss such things so she replied,

"A stork left her under a bush in the garden."

Finally, Tommy sought out his great grandmother who was upstairs in the bedroom.

"Great Grandma," he said softly "where did my grandma come from?"

"Not now darling," she replied, "I'm a bit tired, but you must have heard of the stork?"

The next day in school, the teacher asked the children what they had learned.

"Please miss," said Tommy putting up his hand, "as far as I can see, our family hasn't had sexual relations for three generations."

Marjorie and her 20-year-old niece were in the drawing room when Charles walked in and tripped over the dog.

"Fuck me!" he said angrily.

"Charles!" exclaimed his wife, "do watch your language in front of our niece."

Charles glanced at his niece and replied knowingly, "I'm sure you've heard that expression before, my dear?"

"Oh yes," she said winking, "but not usually in that tone of voice."

"Daddy, Daddy, what are those two dogs doing?" asks the little boy.

"Well son, they're making puppies," replies Dad.

Some time later, the boy passes his parents bedroom and peeps in to find them making love.

"Daddy, Daddy what are you doing?" he asks.

"We're making a baby," Dad replies.

The boy thinks for a moment and then says,

"Dad, can you turn Mum over 'cos I'd rather have a puppy."

"Mummy, Mummy, why is Daddy running zigzag across the garden?"

"Shut up and reload."

Mum sat her young son on her lap and said,

"I have a big surprise for you, sweetheart. You're going to have a baby sister. The stork is bringing her in a few days time."

"Golly, Mum," said the boy, "Dad says there's going to be a baby left under the rose bush and grandma says the hospital is going to give us one. We're going to have bloody kids everywhere!"

A woman was given some deer steaks which she cooked and served for dinner that evening.

"What's this, Mum?" asked the young daughter.

"Why don't you try and guess?" replied Mum.

"Is it beef?"

"No."

"Is it lamb?" asked the son.

"No, try harder."

"I'll give you a clue," said Dad. "It's what your mum sometimes calls me."

"Arrrgh!" screamed the son, spitting out the food. "Don't eat it, sis, it's arsehole!"

The young daughter was passing her parents' bedroom one night when she saw them engaged in some passionate lovemaking. The following morning she asked her father what they had been doing.

"Oh nothing to worry about," replied Dad. "Your mum was having a fit and I was holding her down."

The following week, when Dad came home from work the little girl ran to him and said,

"Oh Daddy, I'm so glad you're back. Mummy had another one of those fits today and the next door neighbour had to hold her down."

"Mummy, mummy, can I lick the bowl, please?"

"No, dear, pull the chain like everyone else."

LUCK

One morning, a bored suburban man wakes up to hear a voice in his head saying,

"Give up this awful life. Sell everything, tell your boss to bugger off and take all your money to Monte Carlo."

The man thinks nothing more of it and goes to work as usual. But the voice keeps coming back.

"Go on, sell up, gamble all your money at Monte Carlo."

No matter what he does, the voice keeps pounding away in his head until he finally breaks. He quits work, sells everything he has and flies out to Monte Carlo where he takes all his money to the gambling casinos. When he arrives, the voice says,

"Go to the roulette table, fifth on the right."

He goes to the fifth table.

"Now put all your money on Black 25."

He puts all his money on Black 25 and the croupier spins the wheel. The ball stops on Red 32.

"Oh fuck," says the voice.

A little girl was up a ladder washing windows. As an old man passed, he noticed she wasn't wearing any knickers and gasped in horror.

"Hey, little girl," he called "here's £10, go and buy yourself some underwear." The little girl ran back inside and told her mother what had happened.

"Really!" exclaimed mum, thinking fast.

"I'll finish the windows," she said, and the next moment she went up the ladder, having removed her knickers first. Lo and behold, the old man passed the woman on the way back from the shops and of course, noticed her lack of underwear.

"Hey, old woman," he called, "here's a quid, go and buy yourself a razor."

The phone rang.

"Colonel Fanshaw," said the adjutant at the other end of the line.

"Your new second-in-command is on his way over to see you. Good chap, but has a weakness for gambling. See what you can do."

Moments later, there was a knock on the door and Lieutenant Hill entered, saluted smartly and waited for his orders. As they were talking, the colonel was taken aback when the lieutenant asked him if he was suffering from testiculitis.

"No, no I'm not," he replied.

But the lieutenant was adamant there was something wrong. He said he could detect it in the way the colonel sat and he would bet £100 he was right.

Thinking this might cure the lieutenant of squandering his money, the colonel agreed to the bet. He then dropped his trousers and revealed all. The lieutenant examined the colonel closely, feeling for any signs of something amiss, and admitted defeat.

"You're quite right, sir", he said, handing over £100. "There's nothing wrong with you."

Later that day the colonel spoke to the adjutant and told him what had happened.

"I'm sure it was a good lesson to learn," he said, "he'll think twice before gambling away so much money again."

However there was a loud groan at the other end of the line.

"Oh no," came the reply, "the sod's done it again! He bet us £500 he'd have you by the balls within an hour of meeting you."

LUCK

The door opened and a huge 6'5" man walked into the pub and up to the bar. He was almost as wide as he was tall with a neck the size of a tree trunk. But, he had a tiny head.

Now the innkeeper was unable to hide his curiosity and addressed the stranger.

"Look, I'm sorry about this but I have to ask. You're such a big man, yet you have such a tiny head. How come?"

The man shook his tiny head in dismay.

"You'll never believe this," he replied "I was walking along the beach last Sunday and I found a magic lamp."

"Why, what happened?" asked the innkeeper, agog.

"Well, I rubbed the lamp and this beautiful genie appeared. She asked me what I wanted and I said I'd like us to have a shag. Well, you would, wouldn't you?" said the big man, confidentially.

"Yeah, yeah," gasped the innkeeper, "so what happened then?"

"She said genies didn't shag so was there anything else, and I said, okay then, how about a little head?"

LUCKY DIP

When human life began, the parts of the body competed against each other as to whom should be boss.

"Well, it's obviously me," said the heart. "I keep all the body working."

"Not at all" replied the brain "I'm the one who controls all the different parts, without me there would be no organisation."

"No, no," said the hands, "we should be boss because we do all the work."

"Rubbish," said the feet, "we should be boss because without us, you wouldn't get around and do all the things you're supposed to do."

Last to speak was the arsehole but everyone else laughed at such an absurd idea. So the arsehole reacted in the only way he could. He blocked himself up. Time went by, the face began to sweat, the eyes began to bulge, the hands clenched and the legs crossed…

"OK, OK," they said in unison, let the arsehole be boss… so the motion was passed and while the rest of the body did all the work, the boss just sat there and passed out the shit! So the moral of this story is: you don't need brains to be the boss, any arsehole will do.

The couple had been married for 20 years and the husband asked his wife how she would like to celebrate their latest anniversary.

"How about a new car for you to get around in?" he suggested.

"No thanks."

"OK, what about a 6-month world cruise, stopping off at all the Seven Wonders of the World?"

"No."

"Well, what would you like?"

"I'd like a divorce," she said.

"What!" he exclaimed, "come on Doris, I wasn't planning to spend *that* much."

A man went to the confessional and told the priest he'd almost had sex with a married woman the night before.

"I don't understand," said the priest, "what do you mean by almost?"

"Well, we rubbed our naked bodies together but I didn't actually put it in."

"Well, in God's sight rubbing together is the same as putting it in, so you will say 20 Hail Marys and put £20 in the collecting box for the poor."

So on the way out, the man went up to the box with his £20 note but after a moment put the money back in his wallet and walked out.

"Hey," said the priest, who had seen this, "why didn't you put the £20 in the box?"

"Well I rubbed the £20 against the box," replied the man, "and in God's sight rubbing is the same as putting it in."

Poor old Jake was lying on his death bed with the dutiful family sitting round, when he suddenly roused himself on smelling his wife's cooking. When she saw him open his eyes, she whispered gently to him, "Jake, my poor man, do you have a last wish?"

"Oh, Mary, that I do," he croaked. "May I just have a small piece of that wonderful cake you're cooking in the kitchen?"

"Oh, no," said his wife, "that's for after the funeral."

The day of the funeral was wet, windy and very stormy. As the mourners left the graveside, there was a tremendous flash of lightning and a deafening clap of thunder.

"Bloody hell!" cursed the new widow. "It didn't take him long to get up there and start pushing his weight around."

"Doctor, doctor," said the simple farmer. "The wife's collapsed out in the field, I think our baby's coming."

As quickly as possible, he showed the doctor his wife laying on the ground moaning.

"I don't think there's time to move her," said the doctor, "we'll have to deliver the baby now. Quick, it's getting dark, shine the light over here."

Within minutes, the baby was born, a fit and healthy 7 lb boy.

"Congratulations!" beamed the doctor. "Let's get them back to the house."

But all of a sudden, the wife began to moan again.

"Quick, bring the light back over," urged the doctor and a minute later another baby boy was born.

"So you have twins," said the doctor happily, "I think this calls for a double celebration."

But again the woman began to moan and again the doctor called for the light. Just in time for another baby boy.

"Well, well, well!" gasped the doctor, "I never expected this!"

"With respect, doctor," said the simple farmer, "do you think it's the light that's attracting them?"

"Let's have some quiet now, children, please," says the teacher.

"Today, we're going to talk about what you'd like to be when you grow up. But first, let's find out what your parents do."

"Jane, what does your father do?"

"He's a doctor miss."

"Very good. Now Matthew, how about your mum?"

"She's a bank manager."

"Good. And you, Jack, what does your dad do?"

"He serves drinks in a brothel, miss."

"That's a wicked thing to say, Jack! How dare you?"

Jack (crying now) "I know, miss, but he's a lawyer, and I'm just so ashamed!"

A young couple get married and on their honeymoon night they retire to the hotel bedroom to consummate the marriage. The man takes off his shirt and the woman notices that his back is covered in small scars. "How did you get those?" she asks.

"When I was eight years old I had the pneesles," he says.

Then the man takes off his trousers and she notices that he has a withered leg.

"What's wrong with your leg?" she asks.

"I had rolio when I was 10," he replies.

Then the man takes his Y-fronts off and she says scornfully, "Let me guess, smallcox!"

Little Red Riding Hood was walking through the forest one day, when she ran into the Three Little Pigs.

"Little Red Riding Hood, beware! The Big Bad Wolf is waiting for you!" they said. "He's gonna pull up your little red dress, pull down your little red panties, and ride your little red socks off!" Little Red Riding Hood nods her head and says, "That's okay," and continues on her way.

A little while later Smokey the Bear comes up to her and says, "Little Red Riding Hood, beware! The Big Bad Wolf is waiting for you! He's gonna pull up your little red dress, pull down your little red panties, and ride your little red socks off!"

Again she nods her head and says, "I'm not worried." and continues on her way. Well she walk on a bit further, and soon the Big Bad Wolf jumps out and says, "Little Red Riding Hood, beware! I've been waiting for you. Now I'm gonna pull up your little red dress, pull down your little red panties, and ride your little red socks off!"

Very calmly Little Red Riding Hood goes into her basket and pulls out a .357 Magnum. Points it straight between the wolf's eyes and says, "No you're not! You're gonna pull up my little red dress, pull down my little red panties, and eat me like the story says!"

A fair is being held in the grounds of a convent to raise funds for the orphan children. One of the attractions is a stall where people can play darts for prizes. Two men pass by and decide to have a wager between them.

"Come on Martin, I bet you £50 you can't get 180 with your next 3 darts."

Now Martin has a reputation for being quite good with the darts, so he readily agrees to the bet. His first dart hits treble twenty, but his second dart only hits a single.

"Ah ha," says his mate, "that's £50 you owe me, you won't get it now."

Martin throws the last dart at the board half-heartedly, it hits the wire and bounces right back hitting a nun in the eye.

As she falls to the ground, he announces in triumph,

"Not so fast, I think you owe me. That's one nun dead and eighty!"

God made Eve and for a while she was very happy in the Garden of Eden, then one day she went to him and said,

"I'm lonely, I'd like a companion."
"Okay," said God. "I'll make you a man and we'll call him Adam. But I must warn you, he'll be flawed. He'll be nasty and aggressive, he'll only pretend to listen to you, he won't see your point of view and he'll pick fights. However, on the good side, he'll have strong muscles, be a competent hunter and be quite good in bed. But I'll only do this on one condition," said God.

"What's that?" asked Eve.

"That you let him believe he was made first."

A woman walked into the ladies toilet to find a man standing there.

"Hey!" she exclaimed, "This is just for women".

"So is this," he said, turning round.

A man is reading the evening paper when his eye catches an advertisement for the biggest John Thomas competition, to be held at his local pub.

"I think I'll have a go at that," he says to his wife.

"Oh no, Terry, don't."

"Why not? I could win £250."

"But I couldn't stand anyone seeing yours it would be so embarrassing."

Nothing more is said but a few days later the wife catches her husband counting out a wad of notes.

"Oh Terry!" she exclaims, "you did go in for that competition. You took it out for everyone to see."

"Oh come on love, don't be so upset. I only took enough out to win."

A man went into the public toilets and saw a bloke without any arms standing at the urinals.

"Do us a favour mate," he said, "can you get my pecker out for me?"

"Yeah, sure," said the man, so he unzipped the blokes flies and aimed his pecker at the porcelain. But as he looked down, he noticed it was red raw with horrible sores all over it and oozing puss. Afterwards, the man zipped up the other's flies but couldn't help remark,

"What's wrong with your willy, it doesn't look right to me."

"I don't know," replied the bloke, "but I wouldn't touch it myself," as he took his arms out of his shirt.

Gregory was determined to improve his social skills so the next time he met 'man-about-town' Harvey Wilkins, he asked him for a good joke that he could tell next time he was in company.

"OK," said Harvey, "here's one. Four separate people spend an afternoon in the park, all meet up at the bandstand. One was a policeman, one was a young woman, one was a horseman and the fourth was a pensioner. Now which of the men knew the woman?"

Gregory looked absolutely dumfounded.

"Well, I have no idea," he stuttered.

"The horse manure," laughed Harvey. "Do you get it – the horseman knew her."

"Oh right," replied Gregory laughing politely but not really understanding. "Thanks Harvey."

The next time Gregory went for a pint in his local, he

was determined to tell the joke and become 'one of the lads'.

"I've got a joke," he said. "There were four people at a bandstand in the park. One was an old pensioner, one was a horseman, one was a policeman and the other was a brunette. Which of the three men knew the brunette?"

"Dunno" came the reply from those listening.

"Well, the answer's 'horse-shit', but I can't think why now."

Two men were talking about their sons over a pint of beer.

"My son must be the laziest bugger in the world," complained Alan. "He never does a thing."

"No," argued Bob. "My son is the laziest."

After discussing this problem for a while, they decide to go to each other's houses to check it out. When they get to Alan's house, they find his son lying on the sofa, watching TV and surrounded by sweet papers.

"Hey, son, pop down the road and get me an evening paper."

"No chance," replied the boy.

"Go on, I'll give you a couple of quid for going."

"Leave me alone, go away," came the reply.

So the two men went over to Bob's house and discovered his son lying on the sofa, watching the TV, the fire full on, the boy dripping with sweat, but also crying.

"What's up, son?" asked his father.

It took a while for his son to answer but eventually he replied, "I can't change channels, dad, the remote's fallen off the back of the sofa."

The angry husband stormed into the pub and confronted a man, quietly drinking at the bar.

"You bastard!" shouted the husband. "Thought you could get away with it, did you? Well, think again. I've got proof right here that you've been carrying on with my wife."

He took some photographs out of his pocket and showed them to the man.

"See," he continued. "This is a picture of you and my wife drinking together in the pub. And this one shows you kissing her in the back of your car...and look at this, in this one she's half undressed. What have you got to say for yourself?"

The man studied each of the photos for a few minutes and then replied,

"I'll take six copies of photo number three."

"My bloody stupid boyfriend is going to die of syphilis!" cried the distraught woman.

"Oh, no," replied her friend. "No one dies of syphilis anymore."

"Well they do, if they give it to me," she retorted.

A man returned from the doctor's with some very bad news. He had been told that his sex life was nearly over because he had simply worn out his tackle.

"I would estimate that you have about 30 sessions left," said the doctor sympathetically.

When the man told his wife she was shocked.

"Oh, no? Only 30 left! We must make every one of these very special. Let's make a plan now."

"I have," he said. "I made a schedule on the way home and your name isn't on it."

When a woman says...

"Come on Shaun, this place is a hovel. You and me need to clean it up. Put away everything lying on the bed, and then all the stuff on the floor ought to go into the washing machine immediately or we'll have no clothes left."

The man hears...

"Na na na you and me na na na on the bed na na na immediately na na na no clothes."

A despicable husband was travelling round the country buying new merchandise for his department store. His trip lasted much longer than usual, so he would keep in touch with his wife by sending her telegrams saying, "Still travelling, still buying".

After two more weeks had passed, the wife eventually sent a message back to him.

'Come home at once or I'll be selling what you're buying!'

A miserly old vicar decided to save money by painting the outside of the church himself. He bought a large can of paint and set to work. But after finishing two walls, he realised he didn't have enough paint to finish. He was determined not to spend any more money so he thinned the paint down with water and just managed to finish the job. Unfortunately, during the night there was a terrific thunderstorm and when he went to inspect the church the following morning, the two walls which had been painted with thinned down paint, had streaked badly.

"Oh what shall I do?" he said in despair, and a voice boomed out from the heavens, "repaint and thin no more."

LUCKY DIP

An atheist was walking through the jungle when he was confronted by a huge lion. He stood rooted to the spot, fear oozing from every pore. The lion growled and got ready to pounce.

"Oh God, please help me," he pleaded.

A voice from the heavens boomed out,

"Help you! You've spent all your life denying my existence, why should I help you now?"

Then the atheist had an idea.

"Please God, if you won't help me, then perhaps you could make the lion a Christian instead."

"Yes, alright," agreed God.

The next minute there was a sudden flash of light and the lion got down on all fours and began to pray.

"Oh thank goodness for that," muttered the frightened man, until he heard what the lion had to say.

"For what we are about to eat may the Lord make us truly thankful."

LUCKY DIP

A man is out practising golf when he hits his ball into a wooded area at the side of the fairway. Muttering to himself, he goes looking for it and stumbles across a funny little gnome sitting cross-legged on the ground.

"Good day to you," says the man, politely.

The little gnome nods his head, then says,

"I see you're not having a good day. I bet you wish you could be the world's greatest golf player?"

"If only," replies the man wistfully.

"Well perhaps I could help you. I have magic powers. But it will mean your sex life will become virtually non existent."

"A champion golfer, instead of a champion lover. Yes please," says the man.

Suddenly, a terrific wind swirls through the trees and the next moment the man is back on the fairway as if nothing has happened. Over the next year, his game goes from strength to strength and he becomes one of the leading golfers in the world.

One day, as he walks the old familiar fairway where his success first began, he steps off into the woods to see if the gnome is still there. Sure enough, he's sitting cross-legged on the ground.

"I hear you're the best in the country," says the gnome.

"But how's your sex life?" he smirks.

"Not so bad," replies the man.

"What!" exclaims the gnome? "What do you mean? How many times did you have sex last year?"

"Oh, I think it was five times."

"And you call that not bad?" sneers the gnome.

"Well, it's not bad for a Catholic priest with a small congregation!"

A man decides he would like to become a monk so he goes along to the local monastery for an interview.

"If you want to be a monk, you have to pass two tests," says the Abbot. "In the first test, you will be put into a locked cell where you will live on bread and water for a year, praying to God and reading the Bible. Then, if you are still determined, you will take the second test. This time, a bell will be hung from your John Thomas and a nude woman will be placed in front of you. If the bell doesn't ring, we will welcome you as one of our brothers. Do you agree to the tests?"

The man agrees and prepares himself for the first test. A year later, he emerges from the cell, still determined to become a monk. So arrangements are made for the second test. A bell is tied to his willy and a beautiful nude woman is placed in front of him. Immediately, the bell starts to ring.

"I'm so sorry," says the Abbot "but I'm afraid you've failed the test."

"Now wait a minute," protests the man. "I defy anyone to pass the second test. I demand to be shown proof."

"Very well," says the Abbot and he calls the other 12 monks into the room, tells them to strip and ties bells to their willies. The naked woman returns and not a bell rings except the poor man who demanded the test. In fact, the bell rings so frantically it falls off onto the floor. As he bends down to pick it up, the other 12 bells begin to ring.

"I hear you were playing golf last Sunday," said the vicar to one of his parishioners.

"Er… yes, that's right," replied the man a little embarrassed, "it's not a sin to play on a Sunday, is it?"

"It is, the way you play it," retorted the vicar.

MADHOUSE

The doctor was on his daily round of the mental asylum and had just entered the room of two of his long-term patients. One was sawing imaginary wood into hundreds of little pieces and the other was hanging upside down from the ceiling.

"What are you doing?" the doctor asked the first man.

"I'm sawing wood," he said, "isn't that obvious?"

"Well what's your friend doing?"

"Oh don't mind him, he thinks he's a light bulb."

"Don't you think you should help him down before all the blood rushes to his head?" continued the doctor.

"What!" exclaimed the man, "and work in the dark!"

The ward sister was doing her rounds in the lunatic asylum when she noticed that one man was racing around the room with his arms spread out making zooming noises.

"Hello Colin," she said, "What are you doing?"

"I'm flying to America," he replied.

Two days later she saw him lying on the ground with

his arms still spread out, but making no noise.

"What's happened now?" she asked.

"I've just landed in America," he replied.

So the ward sister moved on and spotted Gerald sitting down behind his bed, masturbating furiously.

"Now, Gerald, what's going on here?" she said sternly.

"I'm shagging Colin's wife while he's in America," replied Gerald.

MARRIAGE

A wife came home from work to discover her husband crying inconsolably.

"What's wrong?" she asked.

"Do you remember 12 years ago when I got you pregnant and your father threatened to have me put in jail if I didn't marry you?"

"Yes."

"Well today, I would have got out!"

A couple were going through a very rocky time with their marriage so the wife suggested they go and see a marriage counsellor. The man listened intently while the wife told him all the grievances she had towards her husband, particularly the fact that he had lost all interest in her. The counsellor nodded his head in understanding. Certainly the husband had shown no reaction to what was being said. So the counsellor decided on some radical treatment. He went over to the wife, took her in his arms and gave her a long lingering kiss.

"There," he said to the bored husband. "Your wife needs that at least three times a week."

"Okay," he replied. "I'll bring her in Mondays, Wednesdays and Fridays."

"Hello Cyril, what's up?"

"It's the wife. She says she'll leave me if I keep going to all the football matches."

"Oh dear, that's a shame."

"Yes, I shall really miss her."

A middle-aged couple were visiting the local May Day country show and while he went off to the beer tent, she wandered around the livestock area. In the bottom pen stood a mighty bull and a notice on the gate informed the reader that the bull had been out to stud more than 200 times in one year. As she looked up, she caught the owner's eye and recognised him from the local farm.

"Hello Harry, this is a fine beast! You must be very proud. Do me a favour please. If you see my husband tell him about the bull and about him going to stud more than 200 times."

Later on, Harry bumped into the husband and gave him the message from his wife.

"I see," said the husband, "and was this with the same cow every time?"

"Oh no," replied Harry, "two hundred different cows."

"Good. Let my wife know that when you see her."

An elderly couple were driving home late one night when they were stopped by the police.

"Excuse me, madam," said the officer, "this is just to warn you that your brake light isn't working. You need to get it fixed tomorrow."

The old woman cupped her hand over her ear and said: "What did you say?"

The old man shouted in her ear:

"He said the brake light's not working."

"Can I see your driving license?" continued the officer.

"What?" she asked.

"He wants to see your driving license," shouted the old man.

As the officer looked at the license he remarked,

"Oh, I see you come from Bolton. I went there once, met a woman, had the worst sex ever."

"What did he say?" the old woman asked her husband.

"He said he thinks he knows you," came the reply.

The man booked into the 4-star hotel and went up to his room. After having a couple of drinks in the bar and a meal in the restaurant, he returned to his room and rang down to reception.

"Room 205. I'd like a woman up here immediately," he demanded.

"I'm sorry, sir, it's not that kind of hotel," came the reply.

"Oh come on," said the man. "I've paid a lot of money to stay here, and I've been a regular customer for years. Tonight, though, I'm really missing my wife, and I just need someone to take her place for a few hours. What's so bad about that?"

Well, the receptionist was moved by this, so he relented, and got on the phone to a girl he knew would be interested.

An hour or so later there was a knock on the door and the girl entered the room.

The guest looked at her for a moment then said,

"Good, that's fine. Right, get undressed and into bed".

The girl did as he asked and the man did the same.

"Okay," he said, "turn your back to me, tell me you've got a headache and start whingeing."

A woman sat in the waiting room while the doctor examined her husband. Afterwards, he came out to speak to her.

"I'm afraid to say your husband is quite seriously ill. He must be cared for at all times. He must have only the best food, plenty of rest and a spotless house. It'll be quite hard for you to cope because you'll now have to do everything yourself – all the heavy chores and the gardening. But I know you'll think it's worthwhile."

As they drove home later, the husband asked his wife,

"So Doris, what did the doctor have to say?"

"He said you're going to die," she replied.

An elderly couple had met in an old people's home and after a few months the man got down on his knees and asked for the woman's hand in marriage. She gladly accepted.

However, the next morning when the old man woke up, he couldn't remember what the woman's answer had been. Feeling extremely embarrassed, there was no way round it but to ring her up and find out.

"Hello Gloria, it's Cyril," he said. "I feel awfully silly about this but I wondered whether you'd tell me again what your answer was to my marriage proposal. I'm afraid I can't remember!"

"Oh Cyril," she replied happily, "I'm so glad you phoned. I knew I'd said 'yes' to someone but I could not remember who it was!"

"You're going to be really sorry," screamed the wife to her husband. "I'm going to leave you."

He replied: "Well make up your mind, which one's it going to be?"

A newly married couple arrived home from the honeymoon and no sooner had they unpacked, he started laying down some rules.

"Just so you understand," he said, "I'll go out with my mates, when I want and where I want. I don't need permission from you. I also expect clean clothes everyday, a clean and tidy house, and dinner on the table at 6.00 p.m. sharp, whether I'm here or not."

"Okay," she said calmly. "But just let me say this. There'll be sex here every night at 7.30 whether you're here or not!"

"Oh Sharon," said her husband, "I've invited Derek round for supper tonight."

"Tonight!" she shrieked, "but the house is in a terrible mess, the kitchen needs a good clean and the dirty washing's piling up."

"Perfect," he said, "the fool's thinking of getting married."

The young couple arrived home from an idyllic honeymoon and took up married life. But within two days the new bride went round to her parent's house in tears.

"Oh Mum," she sobbed, "he was so wonderful on holiday, but now we've returned home he keeps using four letter words!"

"Oh you poor darling," sympathised Mum. "What's he saying?"

"Dust, cook, wash, iron...!"

A woman went for an eye test and after the examination she was told she had perfect vision.

"Rubbish!" she exclaimed.

"But it's absolutely true" protested the optician. "I can show you the results."

"I do not have perfect vision and I can prove it," she said again. "I can show you my husband."

Said the bitter man to his wife,

"You know, Beryl, you should go braless."

"Really!" she said. "Is that because my breasts are still young and firm, even after all these years?"

"No, it's because they might pull the wrinkles out of your face," he replied.

The small community had been warned for days that the river was swollen and could break its banks at anytime. It happened on a Sunday afternoon and within hours the area was under 6 inches of water. Doris and Ida were sitting on the roof of Ida's bungalow waiting for the waters to recede when suddenly Doris spotted a hat on top of the water. As she watched, the hat would move slowly one way and then come back the other way, over and over again.

"Well, that's odd," she said, pointing the hat out to her friend. "It seems to be moving up and down."

"Oh that's just my Jack," replied Ida, dismissively. "I told him he had to get that lawn mowed today come hell or high water!"

A woman walks into the bedroom to discover her husband packing his bags.

"Where are you going?" she asks.

"To Florida," he replies.

"Why?"

"Somebody told me that every time you make love there, they give you £10."

Immediately, the woman starts packing her bags as well.

"What are you doing?" demands the husband.

"I'm going to Florida."

"Why?"

"I've got to see how you're going to live on just £20 a year," she replies scornfully.

The man leaned over and whispered into his bride's ear, "I love you terribly."

"I know," she replied, "but we've got a lifetime to work on it."

MEN

Why do bankers make the best lovers?

They know the penalties for an early withdrawal.

A husband and wife were having a flaming argument about their money problems.

"If it wasn't for my money, that Porsche and that swimming pool wouldn't be here."

She retorted, "If it wasn't for your money, I wouldn't be here!"

"Hello Josie, you look preoccupied this morning," remarked her friend.

"I am a bit," she replied. "This morning my boyfriend lost all his money on the stock market."

"How awful! You must feel so sorry for him."

"I am. I'm just wondering how he will cope without me."

A man was set upon by muggers as he walked down the dark street. Although there were four of them, the victim put up a good fight but was eventually battered to the ground with broken ribs and a broken nose.

One of the muggers went through his pockets and to his amazement found 54p.

"Hey, why did you put up such a fight for a measly 54p?" asked the mugger.

The poor man gasped in pain, "I didn't know that's all you were after," he moaned. "I thought it was the £200 I had in my shoe."

Every wife likes her husband to have something tender about him, especially legal tender.

A rich young man was involved in a very bad car crash, and his Porsche was a write-off. As he lay stunned at the side of the road, he moaned quietly to himself, "Oh, my car, my poor car".

A paramedic overheard his words and knelt down beside him.

"Excuse me, sir," he said gently, "I think you should be more concerned about your arm."

The young man looked down to where his arm should have been and started to cry in anguish, "Oh my Rolex, my Rolex!"

A woman rushed into the lounge to find her husband asleep on the sofa.

"Quick, Jack, get up. I've just won the £20 million jackpot. Get packing and ring the bus station."

Jack jumped up. "What shall I ask for? What's the destination?"

"I don't care," she replied, "just as long as you're out of here before lunch-time."

What do a man and the tax office have in common?

They're both impossible to get through to when you want to talk.

A man was talking to his mate in the pub about his financial problems.

"It's no good Tony, I'm going to sit down with my wife tonight and tell her a few home truths. She has no idea about money."

The next day they met up again and Tony asked how it went.

"Oh great," he replied, "we've sorted things out. I'm going to give up beer and football."

A very insecure man was anxious to know how much his wife loved him.

"Darling, if I was horribly injured in a car crash and had to spend the rest of my days in a wheelchair, would you still love me?"

"Of course I would, sweetheart," she replied, "I'll always love you."

"And if I lost all my money on the stock market, would you still love me?"

She looked at him for a moment and then said, "Sweetheart, I've told you, I will always love you...and I'll miss you terribly."

MEN

On the eve of his marriage a man was having last-minute doubts.

"Oh Julie, you're not just marrying me because I've inherited £1 million from my late uncle?"

"Of course not," she replied, "I'd marry you no matter who left you the money."

A despicable young man heard that his elderly aunt only had six months to live. Now his aunt was very rich and doted on her two Siamese cats. So the young man decided to curry favour with his aunt, hoping that she would be generous to him in her will.

Every week he would travel to her house and make a big fuss of the cats, feeding them, grooming them and even taking them for walks. Six months went by and the old lady died. Sure enough she remembered him in her will. She left him her cats!

Two tight-fisted men, Graham and Robert, were on a mountaineering holiday in Scotland when Graham slipped badly and ended up hanging by his fingertips over a crevasse.

"Quick, Bob," he screamed, "get down to the village and buy a rope. I don't know how long I can hang on here."

Bob raced off, leaving Graham hanging there and after 20 minutes his grip was beginning to weaken. Then to his relief, he heard Bob returning.

"Hurry up, help me quick," he yelled, "have you got the rope?"

"No," said Bob, "those greedy buggers in the village wanted £10 for it."

A famous Hollywood star was standing naked at the bedroom window doing his exercises. Suddenly his wife came into the room, rushed over to the window and pulled the curtains.

"You idiot," she hissed, "if people see you, they'll think I only married you for your money."

MEN

When do you care for a man's company?

When he owns it.

The young man got down on his knees and said shyly, "Darling will you marry me?" as he offered her a glittering ring.

"Oh my!" she said, looking pleased. "Are they real diamonds?"

"They'd better be," he replied. "Otherwise I've been cheated out of £15."

Little William walks past his parent's bedroom one night and spots them making love. The following morning he asks his dad why they were acting in that way.

"It's because your mother wants a baby," replies dad.

A couple of days later, he sees his mother performing oral sex and later asks his dad why she was doing that to him.

"Because she wants a Porsche," replies dad.

MISERLY

Did you hear about the miser who was so mean, the only way he would take a bubble bath was to eat baked beans the day before?

Did you hear about the miser who lived in Appletree Avenue?

One day, his friend saw him scraping paint off the walls and putting it in a paper bag.

"Are you redecorating?" asked the friend.

"No, I'm moving," was the reply.

A young man went to Las Vegas and won a million dollars on the jackpot. He arrived back in England and rang his parents to tell them the good news.

"And I'll be giving you and mum £100 each," he said.

On hearing this, the parents were very upset and the father, in a moment of rage, told him they were not really his parents.

"What!" exclaimed the young man, "are you telling me I'm a bastard?"

"That's right, and a fucking mean one at that!" came the reply.

An Englishman, Scotsman and a Jew met up in an hotel, and decided to go and have dinner together. They chose an expensive restaurant, and really went to town, with four courses each and the best champagne available. After the meal, the Englishman realised with a sinking heart that he would very likely be landed with the bill. He began to reach for his wallet, when suddenly the Scotsman piped up, "Don't worry about the bill, lads, this one's on me!"

"Thanks very much, very decent of you," replied the others.

They made their way back to the hotel, and the Englishman said goodnight to his companions in the hotel lobby, and went up to bed.

He was on his way into breakfast the following morning, when the newspaper headline caught his eye: "Famous Jewish ventriloquist kicked to death in hotel lobby".

MONEY

A couple parked in Lovers Lane and started necking. As they got more and more aroused, the man began to undo the girl's blouse.

"Wait a minute," she said. "I think I ought to tell you that I'm a prostitute and if you want sex it'll cost you £20."

Feeling angry but beyond the point of no return, he handed over £20 and they carried on.

Much later, once they'd got dressed again, they sat back in the front seats but he didn't start up the car.

"Hey, what's wrong?" she asked.

"Well, I think I ought to tell you that I'm a mini cab driver and until you pay me £25 for the fare, I'm not driving you back into town."

Sky high rates had left the Lord of the Manor badly in need of funds. He said to his wife,

"Cynthia, old dear, times are hard, we're going to have to cut back a bit. If only you'd learn to drive, we could get rid of the chauffeur."

"And if only you'd learn to fuck, we could get rid of the gardeners!" she replied.

A man lost his wallet on a train from Paddington to Penzance. He stood up in the carriage and addressed his fellow passengers.

"Excuse me ladies and gentlemen, may I have your attention please. I've lost my wallet containing £150. If anyone finds it, I will gladly give them £20 reward."

As he finished speaking a voice was heard to say,

"Anyone giving the wallet to me will get £40 as a reward."

"And I'll give £60 to anyone who gives it to me!" said another.

For three weeks a woman had been the main contestant on a national TV quiz show. Time after time, she had defeated every other contender and was only one question away from winning £1 million. On the eve of her big day, nerves were beginning to make her ill so her husband sneaked into the TV studio and found the jackpot question and answer.

"Doris," he said, "tomorrow's question is about the male anatomy and the answer is head, heart and penis."

For the rest of the evening and during the night he asked her the same question every 5 minutes. Alas, her nerves were so bad, she kept forgetting the answer. Ten minutes before the show, he was still instructing her.

"Come on Doris, don't forget, it's the head, heart and penis."

"Head, heart and penis," she kept muttering to herself, as the programme got closer.

"Ladies and gentlemen," announced the quizmaster, "please welcome back Mrs Doris Parsons who is one question away from £1 million."

"Doris, can you name the three main parts of the male anatomy. You have 12 seconds."

There wasn't a sound to be heard as the seconds started ticking away.

"The head," said Doris.

"That's right. 9 seconds left."

"Er… the heart," said Doris.

"Yes!" said the quizmaster, "5 seconds left."

"And… um… er… oh dear, my husband kept driving it into me last night… er… I had it on the tip of my tongue this morning."

The bell went for the end of time.

"Well that's good enough for me," said the quizmaster.

MONEY

A frail old lady of 98 won £3.4m on the lottery. Her family were concerned that the news would shock her so much, it might lead to a heart attack, so they called in the doctor and explained the problem.

He smiled at them kindly and said reassuringly:

"Don't worry about a thing. Although I say so myself, I'm very good at breaking news to people and the old lady's health will not be affected."

The doctor went to see the lady and over afternoon tea, they chatted about all kinds of things until he eventually brought the subject round to money.

"So Mrs Weaver," he said, "what would you do if you won millions of pounds on the lottery?"

"I'd give half to you," she promptly replied.

The doctor dropped dead with shock.

The painter and decorator did a beautiful job on the outside of the house and the husband was so impressed, he gave him extra money.

"Here, take this," said the husband passing him another £50, "take the missus out to dinner."

Later that night, there was a knock on the door and the husband was surprised to see the painter standing there.

"Hello, did you forget something?"

"No," replied the painter. "I've come to take your missus out to dinner."

"Oh John," said his wife at breakfast. "I had a wonderful dream last night, I dreamt you bought me a diamond ring. What do you think it means?"

John replied confidently, "You'll know tonight."

Lo and behold, when John arrived home from work he gave her a book on the meaning of dreams!

A couple were faced with severe financial difficulties and it was decided that she would take up prostitution.

"Charge them £80 if they go the whole way or £30 for a hand job," he said.

So the wife spent a week walking the streets and doing the business. Then one night a man approached her and asked about the price.

"I can't afford to go the whole way so I'll just have a hand job," he said, giving her £30, and smoothly dropping his trousers.

Oh my! When the woman saw how well endowed he was, she ran round to her husband who was waiting in the car and said,

"Derek, have you £50 I could borrow?"

A successful executive decides it's time to make a man of his son so he takes him down to the local brothel. The son disappears into a room with one of the girls while he waits outside – but he can't help listening through the door. Now the son is very well endowed and the girl gasps at the amazing sight. As they begin the business, he takes it very gently but the girl begs for more.

"Just put it in another inch," she says. A little later, she repeats her wish.

"Oh please put in another inch and I'll knock £5 off the price." So he does but still she begs for more.

"Another inch and I'll knock off £10," she informs him.

And so it goes on, the girl is so delighted with the man's performance that she promises to take off more and more money.

"Please, please," she moans till eventually she cries, "a little bit more and it's free, it's free."

Now all this time, the father has been listening outside the door and when he hears this, he bursts into the room and shouts,

"Move over son, leave this to me, it's time to make a profit."

Three men visited a brothel and were told that the price they would pay, would be three times the length of their dick. Afterwards, the first man complained that he'd had to pay £38. The second man said he'd had to pay £30, but the third man smiled and said he'd only paid £6.

"How come?" they asked in astonishment.

"Ah well, you see, after thinking about it, I decided to pay on the way out!"

MOTHERS

It was Saturday night and three sisters were going out with their boyfriends.

"Bye mum," said the first sister, "I'm going out with Chas to listen to jazz."

Moments later the second sister came to say goodbye.

"I'm going out with Lance to dance."

Then the third sister walked in.

"Bye mum, I'm going out with Chuck."

"Oh no!" exclaimed the mother quickly. "You're not going anywhere."

A woman was walking along the street with her blouse undone and her breast hanging out. A passer-by stopped her and said,

"Excuse me Madam, did you realise your blouse is undone?"

"Oh no," she wailed, looking down. "I've left the baby on the train!"

Poor mum! She was tearing her hair out at the behaviour of her young son. Whenever he met anyone he would run up to them, kick them hard on the shins and pinch their backsides.

Eventually mum took him to see a child psychiatrist and as they entered the consulting room, the little boy ran up to the doctor, kicked him hard on the shins and pinched his backside.

Immediately the psychiatrist bent down and whispered in the boy's ear. It had a miraculous effect. The boy turned pale and ran back to his mother, cowering behind here.

"This is wonderful," she enthused, "he's cured! What did you say to him?"

"I told him that if he ever did that again I'd come and find him and smash his fucking face in."

Barbara was pushing her newborn son along the road when she met her old friend.

"Ooh, let's have a look," said her friend, "isn't he beautiful. He looks just like his father."

"Yes, he does, doesn't he?" replied Barbara sadly. "I only wish he looked a bit more like my husband."

MOTHERS-IN-LAW

A man had been out all night on a stag do. They'd ended up watching blue movies so by the time he crawled home about 5 o'clock in the morning, he was as randy as hell. He tore his clothes off, ran upstairs and slid quietly into bed where he roused his wife and spent the next 45 minutes in wild sex.

Later, just before falling asleep he went back downstairs to get a glass of water and noticed someone asleep on the sofa.

"Arrgh!" he wailed, looking down to see his wife. "What are you doing here?"

"Oh hello Jim," she mumbled. "Mother had a headache so I said she could sleep in our bed."

The phone rang.

"Mr. Jones, I'm afraid I have some bad news," said the voice at the other end. Your mother-in-law has died while on holiday in America. Do you know if she wished to be cremated, embalmed or buried?"

"Better safe than sorry," came the reply. "Let's go for all three."

The man ran into work 5 minutes late and immediately bumped straight into his boss.

"Sorry I'm late sir," he panted, "it's the mother-in-law. She's been staying with us and this morning when she went into the kitchen, she slipped, knocked her head and slumped unconscious over the breakfast table."

"Oh my God!" exclaimed his boss. "What did you do?"

"I had to finish my breakfast in the lounge."

"I hate my mother-in-law," said the angry man.

"Oh come on," replied his mate, "if it hadn't been for her, you'd never have met your wife."

"That's what I mean!" he replied with feeling.

MUGS

Late one night, long after the couple had gone to bed, an intruder forced his way into the house. The couple woke to find him standing over them with a gun in his hand.

"I'm going to kill you!" he snarled, "but first, I want to know your names."

The woman said her name was Margaret.

"Margaret," he said dreamily, "why that was my mother's name. I couldn't kill anyone called Margaret."

Then he turned menacingly to the quivering man, "And what's your name?"

"Jack," he replied, "but my friends call me Margaret."

The pregnancy class had just finished and the couples were preparing to leave.

"Just one more thing before you go," said the organiser, "exercise is very important. I'd like to see all the mums-to-be taking daily walks… and I'd like to see their husbands walk with them for encouragement."

For a moment there was silence, then one man asked,

"Is it alright if she carries a golf bag as she walks?"

Three men were sitting on the commuter train going home.

"When I get in, I'm going to pour myself a double whisky, put my feet up and relax" said the first man.

"Well I'm going to strip off, get into the sauna and sweat out all the tension of the day," said the second man.

"And when I get in, I'm going to take the wife's knickers off," said the third man.

The other two looked at him and winked.

"You're a randy old devil," they said laughing.

"No, they're just too tight for me," he replied.

Two motorists are driving towards each other on a narrow country lane. As they slow down to pass each other, the woman sticks her head out of the car and shouts 'pig'.

So the man immediately puts his head through his open window and yells 'bitch'. The incident is over in a second and each continue on their way, except that as the man drives around the next bend he crashes straight into a pig walking in the middle of the road.

How do you impress a woman?

Flatter her, protect her, help her, listen to her hopes and dreams, buy her presents, take her out and wine and dine her, support her and love her.

How do you impress a man?

Turn up naked, bring beer.

What is a perfect man?

One who makes love for hours and then turns into an Indian takeaway.

NEIGHBOURS

A woman popped round to see her new next-door neighbour and found her standing in the hall naked.

"My goodness!" she exclaimed. "What's going on?"

The neighbour explained that she was waiting for her husband to arrive home and she was wearing her love dress.

The woman went home intrigued by what she had seen. She decided to do the same. At 6 o'clock that night, she stripped off and stood in the kitchen waiting for her husband.

"I'm home!" he called out a few minutes later and then gasped in astonishment when he saw his naked wife.

"Carol, what are you doing?" he demanded.

"This is my love dress," she replied sexily.

"Well you could have ironed it first," he replied.

Three women were chatting over mid morning coffee and complaining about the weather.

"It's hopeless," said the first one. "More often than not, I put my washing out and in 5 minutes it starts to rain."

"I agree," said the second. "This morning when I put out my washing, the sun was shining. Now look at it!"

The two women glanced over at their companion who had not said a word.

"Now I come to think about it, you're always lucky when you put washing out. What's the secret?" they asked.

"Well it's quite simple," she replied. "When I wake up in the morning I look at my husband and if his penis is hanging to the left then I know it's going to rain. If it's hanging to the right then I know it's going to be a bright and sunny day."

"Ah ha," interrupted the second woman, "but what if he's got an erection?"

"Well, on a day like that I don't do the laundry."

NEIGHBOURS

It just so happened the two men who lived next door to each other, and didn't see eye to eye, were having their hair cut at the barbers.

"Would Sir like a little hairspray?" said the barber to the first man.

"Good gracious, no," he replied, "if my wife smelled that, she would think I'd been in a brothel."

Overhearing this, the other man said loudly,

"You can put some of that on my hair, my wife's never been in a brothel."

OFFICIAL BUSINESS

"F131," said the voice at the end of the line.

"Good," responded the caller. "I think you ought to know that Martin Carucci of 32 Orchard Garden is growing dope in his woodshed."

Two hours later, the woodshed was raided and all the logs were cut into small pieces in the search for the illegal weed. The next day, Martin received a phone call.

"How did it go?" asked the caller. "Did you get your wood cut?"

"Oh yes," replied Martin. "It's saved me a lot of time."

"Well don't forget, it's your turn to make a phone call next. I'm desperate to get the garden dug over."

There was such a long queue at the ticket office that people were having to wait more than an hour before reaching the counter. Half way down queue D a man suddenly began massaging the shoulders of a bloke standing in front of him.

"What the hell are you doing?" asked the bloke, turning round angrily.

"Well I'm a masseur," explained the man, "and I could see you were very tense so I thought I'd relieve the pressure."

"Well fuck off," replied the bloke. "I'm a tax man, but you don't see me screwing the person in front of me."

The county officials had not known a fire like it for as long as they could remember. The whole paint factory was burning out of control and fire engines from more than 50 miles away had been called to the scene. But still the fire blazed uncontrollably.

Then suddenly, from out of the blue, an old tattered engine arrived from the furthest part of the county. Rarely used, it had stood idle for more than a year but here it was now, heading straight for the blaze. Not for a moment did it ease up, but ploughed on into the heart of the fire and disappeared inside the factory.

Gasps of astonishment were heard from the onlookers, but within minutes it became obvious that by fighting the fire from the centre, the blaze was now under control and soon it was extinguished.

The county officials greeted the fire heroes with smiling faces.

"Men, tonight you showed great courage and determination. Is there any way we can thank you?"

The driver of the truck wiped the soot from his face and replied angrily,

"Yes, you can get the fucking brakes on this thing fixed."

OAPs

A 92-year old man visited the doctor for his six monthly check up. The following week, the doctor bumped into the man walking along the High Street with a flashy woman on his arm.

"I did as you suggested," laughed the man. "Get a hot mamma and be cheerful."

"No, no," said the doctor horrified. "I said you've got a heart murmur. Be careful."

A man stepped into a lift and was taken aback by the awful smell. The only other occupant was a little old lady, and he spoke to her.

"Excuse me, are you suffering from wind?"

"Of course I am," she replied. "You don't think I stink like this all the time?"

Three old men were chatting over a game of dominoes.

"These days I've got such shaky hands," said the first

man, "it's causing me a lot of problems. I went out to prune the roses and cut off all the flowers."

"Oh I know what you mean," nodded the second man. "When I tried to shave this morning, I cut my face to ribbons. See?"

The third man looked at his companions and smiled sympathetically.

"Well just look at the way my hands shake," he said. "Last time I went for a piss, I came three times!"

Two old ladies were sitting on the veranda enjoying the last few minutes of daylight before retiring to bed. One of the ladies turned to her friend and said,

"Nancy, do you still get horny?"

"Oh yes," she replied.

"So what do you do?"

"I suck a lifesaver," she said.

After a few moments silence came the question.

"But who drives you to the beach?"

The doctor had an appointment at the local old people's home to check on three women and test them for dementia.

"Okay Mrs Brownley, can you tell me what four plus four equals?" he asked gently.

"940," she replied.

So he asked the second woman the same question.

"March," came the reply.

The doctor sighed and turned to the third woman.

"Hello Doris, can you tell me what four plus four equals?"

"Yes," she replied immediately, "it's eight."

"Correct" said the doctor, happily, "well done Doris."

"Oh it was easy," she replied. "I just added 940 to March."

The old man said to the doctor,

"Do you think I'll live another ten years?"

"Do you drink?" asked the doctor.

"No."

"Do you smoke?"

"No."

"Do you have sex?"

"No."

"Then what do you want to live another ten years for?"

An old couple had retired to bed and the woman was feeling a bit frisky.

"Oh Harold," she said. "Sometimes it feels just like yesterday that you would put your arm around me as we lay in bed. Where's all that romance gone?"

So the old man, to keep her happy, put his arm around her.

"And then, you used to kiss me," she continued.

The old man sighed, turned over and kissed her.

"And then, do you remember," she said excitedly, "you used to nibble my ears?"

At that, the old man got out of bed and walked to the door.

"Harold!" she called, sitting up in alarm, "where are you going?"

"Just to the bathroom to get my teeth!"

Two old men were sitting in the park watching all the pretty girls go by in their skimpy clothes.

"Phwooarr! God, just looking at them makes me want to sit them on my knee and kiss and cuddle them," said the first man drooling.

"Mmm," agreed the other, nodding, "but wasn't there something else we used to do as well?"

An old man was watching television in his hotel room when a beautiful young girl walked in.

"Oh dear!" she exclaimed blushing, "I'm so sorry, I think I'm in the wrong room."

The old man shook his head sadly and replied,

"No, no my dear, you're in the right room – you're just forty years too late!"

An old woman of 70 had a baby and when she arrived home, she was greeted by lots of friends and relations, eager to see the new arrival.

"When can we see it?" they asked.

"Soon," she replied.

"Can we see it now?" they asked again, 30 minutes later.

"Very soon," she replied.

However another 30 minutes passed and everyone was getting very impatient.

"When can we see the baby?" they said irritably.

"When it cries," she replied.

"But why? Why do we have to wait until it cries?"

"Because I can't remember where I put it," she replied.

An old man was driving down the M1 when his car phone rang.

"Oh Charles, dear," said his wife on the other end of the line, "there's just been a traffic item on the news. They say a car is travelling the wrong way down the motorway, please be careful."

"Hell Louise, it's not just one car, it's hundreds of them!" he replied.

PARENTS

Mum was tidying up her son's bedroom when she discovered an S&M magazine under his bed.

"Oh Ron," she said, showing it to her husband. "What shall we do?"

"Well I don't think spanking him would be a good idea," he replied.

Mum walked into the kitchen wearing her beautiful new fur coat.

"Isn't it fabulous?" she said to her daughter. "What do you think?"

"Oh Mum," replied the girl, "some poor dumb beast suffered so you could have that."

"Dorothy!" exclaimed her mum. "Don't talk about your father like that."

A beautiful baby boy was born to a joyous couple. He was perfect in every way except he didn't cry or make any noise at all. Although this concerned the parents, the doctors assured them that there was nothing wrong with his vocal chords. For some reason, he just didn't want to speak. And so it continued throughout his early life. He grew up normally but just never spoke.

Then, at the age of seven, he was sitting in the kitchen having tea when his mother passed him a glass of juice.

"I haven't tried this flavour before," she said. "I hope you like it."

The boy took a sip and replied, "Ugh, it's horrible, I prefer the other sort."

"Oh my goodness!" exclaimed the mother, looking at him open-mouthed, "you spoke. Why have you never spoken before?"

He replied, "Well up to now, everything's been fine."

"Sharon," said her mum angrily, "I found a condom under your bed. Are you sexually active?

"No," replied her daughter. "I just lie there."

The leader of the Hells Angels and his equally tough girlfriend had a baby son.

A few months after the birth, the father rushed out looking for his girlfriend.

"Hey, honey, guess what?" he said proudly. "Our son's just spoken his first half-word. He said mother."

Over the years, Louise had taken many men home to meet her parents but they had all failed to pass the test.

Her latest boyfriend was Ernie and she was determined that nothing should go wrong, no matter what it took.

"So where do you live?" asked her father.

"I've got a flat near the park," Ernie replied.

"A flat near the park!" snorted Louise in disbelief.

"Dad, he has a penthouse overlooking half of London."

"Do you have a good job?" asked her mum.

"It's quite interesting," said Ernie. "I work in a bank."

"Work in a bank!" laughed Louise, "he's only the top man in their investments department.

At that moment, Ernie started to cough.

"Oh dear, have you got a bad chest?" asked mum.

"Bad chest? No way!" said Louise hysterically, "he's got pleurisy."

The phone rang and Matthew picked it up.

"Son, it's your father here. I'm afraid I'm divorcing your mother."

"What! Dad, you can't! You've been together 40 years!" exclaimed the shocked son.

"It's no good, I'm going to see a solicitor tomorrow," said dad.

"But let me speak to mum," wailed the boy.

"No, not now. She can't come to the phone."

"Listen, dad, don't do anything till I see you, please. I'll drive up tomorrow."

"Well… alright, but will you tell your sister, this is all too painful."

With that, Matthew's father rang off.

Half an hour later, the phone rang and dad picked it up.

"Dad, it's me," said Matthew. "I've spoken to Claire and she's coming with me so we'll be with you at tea time."

Dad put down the phone and turned to his wife.

"Well it's worked. They're both coming tomorrow, though I don't know what we'll do next year to get them to visit."

PARTIES

A woman went to the Fancy Dress Ball dressed all in red – red stockings and suspender belt, red panties and red bra.

"How shall I announce you?" asked the doorman.

"I'm Dying Embers," she replied, "and if I don't get a poke soon, I'm going out."

Early one Saturday night the local vicar called round to see one of his parishioners only to find a party in full swing. As he walked into the front room, he was astonished to find a circle of naked men and a group of blindfolded women moving amongst them, feeling their todgers. The host explained that the women had to guess the name of the man by feeling his genitals.

The vicar blushed and replied,

"Oh dear, I really don't think I ought to be here."

"Nonsense Vicar!" replied the host, "your name has been mentioned twice already."

A pair of Siamese twins joined at the shoulders, lived at the bottom of the street, one loved singing and the other loved shagging. One morning the music twin exclaimed, "A world famous baritone is going to be singing here next month. Let's get tickets, I'd just love to see him!"

So on the night of the concert, the Siamese twins took their seats in the front row. The singer twin sat there enthralled as she listened to his voice while the other twin spent her time pouting at him seductively. Now this didn't go unnoticed by the baritone who invited them round to his dressing room after the show. While the singing twin serenaded them, the other two shagged all over the room in every conceivable position. So, a year went by and posters began to appear, advertising a return visit by the world famous baritone.

"Let's go again and get invited round for another party," said the sex mad twin.

"No, I don't think so," said the singing twin, "I doubt he'd even remember us."

PARTIES

An elephant and an ant fell in love at first sight and spent a night together in the throes of passion. Sadly, when the ant woke up the next morning the elephant had died.

"Oh no!" exclaimed the ant. "One night of passion and I spend the rest of my life digging a grave!"

PEEPING TOMS

The clock strikes 11 o'clock. Snow White yawns and tells the seven dwarfs that she's off to bed. As soon as she goes upstairs, the dwarfs run outside, get on each other's shoulders until the one at the top is able to see through her bedroom window. This night it happens to be Bashful.

"She's just taking her blouse off," he whispers to the dwarf below him.

"She's taking her blouse off," the second says to the third and so the message is relayed down the line.

"Now she's taking her bra off," whispers Bashful.

"She's taking her bra off, she's taking her…" and so the message goes down the line.

"She's taking her skirt off…"

"She's taking her knickers off…"

"She's absolutely naked… Naked… Naked…"

Suddenly, Happy hears someone moving about in the bushes.

"Someone's coming!" he whispers.

"And me… And me… And me… And me…"

268

PENIS

A man was riding through the desert when he saw an Indian lying naked on the ground with his penis sticking up in the air.

"What are you doing?" he asked.

"Me telling time," the Indian replied and sure enough his willy acted like a sundial, casting a shadow across his body. "It's 4 o'clock," he said. A little further on, he saw another Indian lying naked on the ground, with his penis sticking up in the air.

"Me tell time," said the Indian as the man rode by. "It's 6 o'clock," he said. Then 5 minutes later, he saw a third Indian lying naked on the ground but this one was masturbating. To hide his embarrassment, the rider remarked,

"Telling the time are you?"

"No, winding watch," came the reply.

A woman was up a ladder mending some loose tiles on the roof of the house while her husband was sunbathing in the garden. Suddenly, the next door neighbour popped his head over the fence and said,

"Fancy letting your wife do that kind of work. You really are lazy. You should be damned well hung."

"But I am," he replied, "that's why she doesn't complain about doing jobs like these."

Three men walk into a pub in the rough quarter of the city and order 3 pints of beer. Watching them is a group of thugs in the corner.

"Come on," says one, "let's have some fun."

The leader of the thugs swaggers over to the newcomers and says in a loud voice,

"Hey, you three, this is our pub and we're a bit choosy about who drinks in here. So here's what we're going to do. If your three dicks add up to 22" between you then we'll pay for your pints… If not, then me and my mates are going to beat the shit out of you."

The three men at the bar get their dicks out and put them on the counter. The first man's measures 11", the second 10" and the third, 1".

Disgruntled, the thugs pay up and walk away.
"Phew," says the first man, "it's a good thing mine was 11" or we'd have been in trouble."

"Now wait a minute," complained the second, "My 10" was just as important."

"Lads, lads," says the third man, "I'm the one who got us out of trouble. If I hadn't had a hard on, we wouldn't be sipping these beers now."

A man went to the tattooist to have something special done for his wife.

"How about 'I love you' tattooed on your John Thomas," said the shop owner.

The man agreed and that night in bed he revealed all to his wife.

"How about this darling," he said proudly.

"What a surprise," she said scornfully, "trying to put words in my mouth again."

The doctor and his medical students were on their ward rounds when they came to Mr. Biggun's bed. On examining him, they discovered he had the biggest penis they'd ever seen.

"Goodness!" exclaimed one of the students "what's it like when it's reduced?"

"It's down now," replied the man.

"Then what on earth is it like when it's extended?"

"I don't know," replied the man sadly.

The group sympathised with him for being unable to get it up.

"No, no, you don't understand," he protested. "I mean I've never seen it when it's up. Every time I get a hard on, I pass out."

"Doctor, doctor," said the worried young man. "I'm hoping to get married soon but I'm embarrassed about my small penis."

"Oh, we can soon cure that," replied the doctor. "Just visit a farm everyday for the next month, dip your penis in milk and have a calf suck it off."

A few weeks later, the doctor bumped into the man in the street.

"Hello there, how's your marriage?"

"Oh I didn't get married in the end," replied the man. "I bought the calf instead."

A man went to the doctors complaining that there was something wrong with his penis.

"Oh dear, oh dear, oh dear," said the doctor shaking his head sadly. "I'm afraid it's bad news. This penis has just worn out. It's been over used and there is nothing I can do about it. So you'll only be able to have sex another 25 times."

When the man returned home, he told his wife the bad news. She was very kind and sympathetic to his plight.

"We'll certainly have to make the best use of these last 25 times," she said. "You'll have to have the best sex ever."

"I'm glad you said that," he replied, "because I made a list on the way home and I'm afraid there isn't room on it for you."

Every Thursday four men would meet at the sports centre for a game of squash. Afterwards three of them would shower and then go to the bar for a few drinks but the fourth always made some excuse and dashed away. Eventually one of the other three men took him aside and asked him why he never joined them.

"Well, to be honest," said the man blushing furiously, "I'm embarrassed about my willy. "It's so small."

"But does it work?" he was asked.

"Oh yes."

"Then how about swapping it for one that looks good in the shower?"

A woman was cleaning the public toilets when she discovered that someone had drawn a penis on the wall. She got a wet cloth and rubbed it off, only to discover the next day that a larger one had been drawn in its place. So, for a second time she rubbed the drawing off.

However on the third day, she discovered the drawing of the penis was now taking up most of the wall and underneath was written.

"Don't you know, the harder you rub it, the bigger it grows."

He picked her up at a nightclub and invited her back to his place. Nothing much was said on the way back so when they got there she remarked,

"You haven't got much to say for yourself."

"No. I do all my talking with this," he said dropping his trousers.

The girl walked forward and squinted,

"Bloody hell, don't tell me that's all you've got to say?"

Dave and Pete were lined up at the urinals and Dave couldn't help but notice how well endowed his mate was.

"Wow!" he exclaimed, "that's a remarkable piece of equipment you have there."

"Yeah," replied Pete, "It wasn't always like that. I wasn't happy with the one I had, so I went to this exclusive private clinic and had a transplant. It cost £1,500 but it was worth it."

Now Dave couldn't stop thinking about this so a few weeks later, he got the address from Pete and booked into the same clinic. The next time they met, he smiled at his mate and said,

"I think you were had, my new todger only cost £750."

"What!" exclaimed Pete. "Same place, same doctor? Let's have a look."

Dave showed off his new possession and Pete creased up with laughter.

"Oh that's alright," he said, "no wonder it didn't cost so much, it's my old one."

POLICE

A man was speeding through town when he saw a police car coming up behind him with the siren blaring. The motorist put his foot down immediately and the speedometer was touching 80 as he turned into the High Street.

'Oh shit,' he said to himself, 'this is no good' so he slowed down and pulled over.

The police car drew up behind the car and an officer got out to speak to him.

"Did you realise you were doing 80 miles an hour in a 30 mile an hour zone?" he asked.

The man replied,

"I'm sorry, officer, you see my wife ran off with a copper a few months ago and when I saw you chasing me, I thought you were trying to give her back."

Patrick Murphy went for an interview to be a policeman. The kindly sergeant decided to try and put the man at ease by asking him a simple question.

"Now, Mr. Murphy, can you tell me who killed Jesus Christ?" he asked.

Patrick started to sweat heavily and look worried.

After a moment the sergeant continued,

"I can see this is a bit of an ordeal for you. Why don't you go and have a cup of tea and think it over. Pop back in 15 minutes."

Patrick went off to the canteen where he saw his friend Sean who greeted him warmly.

"So me old mate," he said, "how's it going?"

"Great," replied Patrick, "I'm on my first case already."

PRATS

An arrogant young man was setting up a computer system for one of the pretty secretaries.

"Now you're going to need a password," he said, and hoping to embarrass her, he typed in the word PENIS.

However, she had the last laugh when the screen flashed back the message 'password rejected, not long enough.'

"Hey darling," said the prat, "do you want to play magic?"

"What's that mean?"

"You come to my house, we fuck and then you disappear."

The arrogant man sidled up to the beautiful woman in the nightclub and said,

"Hey, gorgeous, the word tonight is 'legs'. How about coming back to my place to spread the word!"

A real sleaze-bag walked into a bar and sat down next to a very attractive woman. He ordered a drink and for the next five minutes sipped at it slowly, continuously looking at his watch.

The woman was so intrigued she finally spoke.

"Excuse me, I couldn't help noticing you keep looking at your watch. Has your date not turned up?"

"Oh no," he replied, "It's nothing like that. I'm looking at this special watch I've just bought. It talks to me."

"Really! What's it saying?"

"It says you're not wearing any knickers," he replied.

"Well it's wrong," she retorted somewhat taken aback.

"Oh damn," he cursed, "it must be an hour fast."

A man walked into a bar and ordered a beer from the very attractive barmaid. He engaged her in conversation.

"I bet I can bite my own ear," he said, putting £5 on the bar.

She accepted the bet and the next moment, he took out his false teeth and nipped his ear. He picked up his winnings and then said,

"I'll give you another chance. For another £5, I bet I can keep an eye on my beer while I go to the loo."

The barmaid hesitated. She didn't want to lose any more money but she knew the toilets were outside.

"Okay," she said, "you're on."

The man took out his glass eye and put it by his pint as he went outside for a pee. Again he collected the money, smiled at her and said,

"Listen, I'll give you a chance to win back all your money. I bet I can make love to you so gently, you won't feel a thing."

She agreed immediately. There was no way she wasn't going to feel him. They disappeared into the storeroom and got down to it on the floor.

As he thrust in and out, she declared with glee. "I can feel it, I can feel it."

"Oh well," he gasped, continuing his humping. "You win some, you lose some."

PUBS

The local bar was so sure that its bartender was the strongest man around that they offered a standing £500 bet. The bartender would squeeze a lemon until all the juice ran into a glass, and hand the lemon to a patron. Anyone who could squeeze one more drop of juice out would win the money. Many people had tried over time, even a weightlifter once, but nobody could do it.

One day a scrawny little man wearing thick glasses and polyester suit came in, and said in a squeaky voice, "I'd like to try the bet."

After the laughter had died down, the bartender said okay, grabbed a lemon and started squeezing. Then he handled the shrivelled remains to the little man.

The crowd's laughter was silenced as the man clenched his fist around the lemon – and six drops fell into the glass.

As the crowd cheered, the bartender paid the £500, and asked the little man, "What do you do for a living? You must be an arm-wrestler or something!"

The man replied, "I work for the Inland Revenue."

Two men talking in a pub.

"Your round," said one.

"Yeah! Well you're a fat bastard as well," replied the other.

A man walked into a pub and ordered 13 pints of beer. As the publican lined them up along the bar, he drank the first, the third, the fifth, the seventh, the ninth, the eleventh and the thirteenth. Then he pocketed his change and got up to leave.

"Hold on," said the publican, "aren't you going to drink the rest?"

"No thanks," said the man. "My doctor ordered me only to have the odd drink."

A pile of dog shit had been deposited on the pavement right outside the entrance to the pub. As the little man walked in, he slipped on it and skidded across the floor. Moments later, a big burly man came in and slipped on the shit as well.

"I just did that," said the small man.

So the big man beat him up.

A bloke with more money than sense went into a pub and threw down a challenge to the customers.

"If anyone can drink 20 pints of Murphy's straight off, then I'll give them £200. Look here it is on the bar."

Everyone shook his head except one man who left the bar.

Disappointed, the bloke was just picking up his money when the man who had left suddenly reappeared.

"Leave your money where it is," he said, "I'll take up your challenge."

Then to everyone's amazement, he downed the 20 pints, one after another, and picked up the £200.

"So why did you go out?" asked the bloke

"Well first I had to go to the pub next door to make sure I could do it!" he replied.

QUICKIES

You know things are bad when you fake an orgasm while masturbating.

What's the difference between a woman and a coffin?

You come in one and go in the other.

How do you know when you've met the man of your dreams?

You trip over his willy in the pub.

The best thing about a blow job is the 10 minutes of silence.

What's the best thing about self abuse?

You don't have to look your best.

What do you get when you cross a donkey with an onion?

A piece of ass that'll bring tears to your eyes.

Did you know that if you're having a bad day, it takes 42 muscles to frown but only four to extend the middle finger and tell them to piss off?

Have you heard there's a new bra on the market called a Sheepdog?

It rounds them up and points them in the right direction.

Did you hear about the ward sister nicknamed Appendix?

All the surgeons took her out.

Why does a Scotsman wear a kilt?

So the sheep won't hear the zipper.

Do you know what happened to the man who had a mole on his willy?

He was reported to the R.S.P.C.A.

What did the cannibal do after he'd dumped his girlfriend?

Wiped his arse.

QUICKIES

What's the difference between a wife and a mistress?

Night and day.

What does a female reindeer do on New Year's Eve?

She goes out to blow a few bucks.

What's the difference between a pay cheque and a penis?

You never have to persuade a woman to blow your pay cheque.

If you call nuts on a wall 'walnuts' and nuts on your chest 'chestnuts', then what do you call nuts on your chin?

A blow job!

QUICKIES

Why did the simple man not enjoy his honeymoon?

He was waiting for the swelling to go down.

Why did the Irishman ask for a refund on his tie?

It was too tight around his neck.

Did you hear about the girl who asked her boyfriend to kiss her somewhere dirty?

He drove her to a coal mine.

What do christmas trees and priests have in common?

The balls are just for decoration.

Why do nymphomaniacs drive cars with sunroofs?

There's more legroom.

Did you hear about the woman who was so ugly, the only people who ever asked her to go to bed were her parents!

Here follows a lesson on ornithology:

What bird is associated with stalking and aggression?

The eagle.

What bird is associated with love and peace?

The dove.

What bird is associated with children?

The stork.

What bird is associated with larceny?

The jackdaw.

What bird is associated with birth control?

The swallow.

Men are like cement. After getting laid, they take ages to get hard.

What do you get when you cross a piranha with a prostitute?

Your last blow job.

Why are puppies like near-sighted gynaecologists?

They both have wet noses.

What did the hurricane say to the palm tree?

Hang onto your nuts; this is no ordinary blow job.

Did you hear about the constipated maths teacher?

He worked it out with a pencil!

What has two grey legs and two brown legs?

An elephant with diarrhoea.

"Hello," said the woman, "are you a pole vaulter?"

"Why yes I am a Pole!" he exclaimed in astonishment, "but how did you know my name is Walter?"

How does a Welshman find a sheep in long grass?

Very satisfying.

What's the different between an oral and a rectal thermometer?

The taste.

Why do the Irish have potatoes and the Arabs have oil?

Because the Irish had first choice.

Did you hear about the man who went into a bank and asked the teller to check his balance?

She pushed him!

What does a dog do, that a man steps into?

Pants.

REAL MEN

How many real men does it take to change a light bulb?

None. Real men aren't afraid of the dark.

A cowboy rides into a rough frontier town and walks into the saloon.

"I'll have a shot of whiskey," he demands from the barman and downs it in one gulp. After another couple of drinks, which he takes more slowly, he leaves the saloon only to return seconds later shouting at the top of his voice:

"Whichever one of you damned critters stole my horse, if it's not back by the time I've had another drink, I'll do what I did in Coyote Creek."

So the man has another drink and goes back outside to see his horse has been returned.

As he mounts to ride away, the barman comes rushing up to him.

"Hey, mister, just out of interest, what did you do in Coyote Creek?"

"I had to walk home," replies the man.

"Bob," whispered his wife urgently, "I think I can hear someone moving around downstairs. Are you awake?"

"No," he replied.

The man was so henpecked, he had to wash and iron his own apron.

What do men and rolls of carpet have in common?

Lay them properly the first time and you can walk all over them for the rest of their lives.

The man behind the bar said to Colin:

"You really are a typical example of a spineless, henpecked man."

"Now look here," replied Colin, "you wouldn't say that if my wife was here."

"Darling," said the husband, "what's your favourite sexual position?"

"Across the street," she replied.

The best way to get a man to do something is to suggest he's far too old to do it.

What is the smartest thing a man can say?

"My wife says..."

Women – what have you got when you have two little balls in your hand?

A man's undivided attention.

What's the difference between pink and purple?

The woman's grip.

A man who had pleaded not guilty beforehand was now in court watching the jury of nine women and two men take their seats. All of a sudden he turned to his barrister and whispered frantically in his ear.

"Your Honour," said the barrister rising, "my client would like to change his plea to guilty."

"And may I ask why he has changed his mind?" demanded the judge.

"Of course. When he pleaded not guilty he didn't realise there would be so many women on the jury. He tells me he can't fool one woman so there's no chance he'd fool nine of them."

"Is your husband easy to please?"

"I don't know, I've never tried."

"Well, isn't that a coincidence?" she said. "You look just like my fourth husband."

"Fourth!" he gasped. "How many have you had?"

"Three."

Women's Lib is making him sleep on the wet bit.

Our dad thinks he wears the trousers in our house, but it's mum who tells him which pair to put on.

No man is really successful until his mother-in-law admits it.

The henpecked husband said he couldn't bear to sit through porno movies.

"Why not?" asked a mate.

"Because I can't stand to see one guy enjoying himself more in ten minutes than I have in twenty-five years."

Many a wife has helped her husband to the top rung of the ladder – and then left him there for a while until she's decided whether the picture would look better somewhere else.

The President of the world's most successful international business, accompanied by his wife, stop for petrol at a small out-of-the-way garage.

As the garage attendant comes out to help them, the wife looks up and screams with pleasure.

"John, oh, no! I can't believe it!" She jumps out of the car and rushes to embrace him.

After a few minutes of animated conversation, she returns to the car looking very thoughtful.

As they drive off, the husband looks at her with interest and asks, "Who was that, sweetheart?"

"That was an old boyfriend of mine. We were together a long time. In fact, we almost got married."

There is a moment's silence and then he says, "Ah, well. I guess you're glad you married me instead."

"What makes you say that?"

"Because I'm the President of an international company."

"That's quite irrelevant," she replies with scorn. "If I'd married John, he would now be President."

"Doctor, doctor, can you come round and see my wife as soon as possible? She is so ill. I had to carry her downstairs to make my dinner."

A wife rang up her husband in anguish.

"Jack, Jack, the doctor says I'm pregnant. Why didn't you use a condom?"

"But I always use a condom," he argued. "Anyway, who is this?"

"If I say no to going to bed with you, will you really commit suicide?"

"Well, that's my usual procedure, yes," he said.

Did you hear about the innocent young girl who met a man in a raincoat?

Later, she recounted the event to her friend.

"Coming back from the supermarket, a man stopped me and showed me the lining of his raincoat."

"That's odd," mused her friend. "Are you sure he only wanted you to see his raincoat?"

"Oh yes, he wasn't wearing anything else."

When man was first made, he only had twenty years of normal sex life. To him, this was horrifying. Meanwhile, the monkey had also been given twenty years normal sex life but he said he only needed ten years, so he gave the other ten to the man.

Likewise, the lion, also with twenty years, gave ten years to the man as well. He agreed that ten years was plenty.

Finally the donkey, agreeing with the other animals that ten years was enough, gave the man another ten years.

So all this explains today's modern man. He has twenty years of normal sex life, ten years of monkeying around, a further ten years of lion about it and finally ten years of making a complete and total ass of himself.

After their honeymoon, the husband brought his wife breakfast in bed. On the tray was fresh orange juice, cereal, bacon and egg, toast and coffee.

"Mmm, thank you darling," she said. "This looks lovely."

"Good," he replied, "because that's how I want it every morning."

A young newly wed girl was telling her friend how she had been teaching her husband to have better manners.

Suddenly she was interrupted by him rushing into the room and shouting,

"Come on, love, how about a quickie?"

Shocked, the girl's friend remarked, "I thought you were teaching him better manners?"

"I am," she stressed. "A month ago, he wouldn't have asked."

RELIGION

Recently a teacher, a bin man, and a lawyer wound up together at the Pearly Gates. St. Peter informed them that in order to get into Heaven, they would each have to answer one question.

St. Peter addressed the teacher and asked, "What was the name of the ship that crashed into the iceberg? They just made a movie about it."

The teacher answered quickly, "That would be the Titanic."

St. Peter let him through the gate.

St. Peter turned to the bin man and, thinking that Heaven didn't REALLY need all the odours that this guy would bring with him, decided to make the question a little harder: "How many people died on the ship?"

Fortunately for him, the trash man had just seen the movie, and answered, "1,228."

"That's right! You may enter into Heaven!"

St. Peter then turned to the lawyer. "Name them."

RELIGION

A priest walked into a pub and addressed the man standing at the bar.

"You, Seamus, do you want to go to heaven?"

Seamus nodded.

"Then come and join me," said the priest, "join me over here."

Eventually all the men had joined the priest except Paddy.

"What's wrong, don't you want to go to heaven?" asked the priest.

"I do, Father," replied Paddy, "but I'm too young to be going just yet."

When you see a priest you call him Father. When you see a Bishop, you call him Your Grace. When you meet a Cardinal it's Your Eminence, and when you see a gorgeous man, it's oh My God!

A couple had been trying for children for many years without any luck. One day their parish priest told them that he was going to Rome for five years but that while he was there he would pray everyday for them and keep a lighted candle in St. Peter's.

So a few years went by and eventually the priest returned home. He went round to see the couple and as he walked up the garden path, he spotted a pair of twins playing on a swing. As the door of the house opened, he saw the poor harassed woman, heavily pregnant, with two small babies in her arms.

"Why Father!" she exclaimed, "we didn't know you'd returned."

"Yes, a week ago," he replied, "and I thought I'd come round to see how you are. I see you've been blessed with children. Where's your husband?"

"He's gone to Rome," she replied, "to blow out that bloody candle!"

The Pope flies to New York for a very important conference but the plane is late so he hasn't got much time. He flags down a cab and gives the driver the address as they move out into heavy traffic.

The Pope looks at his watch in exasperation.

"Can't you go faster?" he asks.

"Oh no," replies the cabbie, "I could lose my license."

Another ten minutes go by and they are still miles from the conference venue.

"I've got a good idea," says the Pope, "let me drive, then if we get stopped, it won't be your fault."

The two men change places, the Pope grabs the wheel, puts his foot down on the accelerator and away they go. All of a sudden, sirens are heard and a police car flags them down.

"Excuse me Sir," says the officer, "did you realise you were well over the speed limit?"

"Yes, I'm very sorry," replies the Pope, "but we have to get to a very important conference in less than 15 minutes."

"Well, in that case follow me," says the officer, and the two cars take off at speed.

"Lieutenant," says the officer, reporting in on the radio. "I'm escorting a very important person to that big conference down town."

"Who's that then?" asks a voice over the mike.

"Don't know, sir," replies the officer, "but he must be a big shot 'cos the Pope's driving him!"

A man was seriously ill in hospital so his family called their priest to offer him comfort. As the priest stood at the side of the bed the man started thrashing around frantically and turning blue.

"I think he wants to tell us something," said the priest, "get him a piece of paper."

Within moments, he'd written something on the paper and handed it back to the priest but before it could be read, the poor man had died.

Some time later, as the bereaved family left the hospital, the priest suddenly remembered the piece of paper that he'd put in his pocket.

"I think it may be the right time to read his last words," said the priest. "It says, get off the fucking oxygen pipe, you're standing on it."

A man was in the park practising penalty taking. He kicked straight at the net but the ball flew up right over the top.

"Dammit, I missed," he cursed.

Just then a priest was walking past and on hearing the man's words, he stopped to speak to him.

"Do not curse," he said, "God is listening."

"Bugger off," replied the man "What's he going to do anyway, send a thunder ball down to get me?" he sneered.

All of a sudden there was a mighty boom from the skies and a huge shaft of fire hurtled to the ground, killing the priest stone dead.

"Dammit, I missed," boomed a voice from above.

A disillusioned priest addressed his congregation one Sunday morning before the service started.

"I have, in my hands, three sermons," he said. "The first costs £200 and lasts four minutes. The second costs £100 and lasts fifteen minutes or the third costs £30 and lasts 65 minutes. Before I continue, we'll take the collection to see which sermon I should use today."

RELIGION

A middle-aged couple had drifted apart and the end of their marriage came one Friday night over a plate of fish and chips.

"It's no good Sonia, this marriage is a sham, I'm leaving you. I may be 57 years old but I've met a 19 year old girl who wants to be with me and I want to be with her," said the husband proudly.

"Well, well, well," replied the wife scornfully. "She's welcome to you. By the way, I've met a gorgeous young man of 19 who goes for older women. I may be 57 as well but he says I've got the body of a 25 year-old. So stuff you, Bob, and just remember this. 19 goes into 57 a lot more times than 57 goes into 19!"

REVENGE

A husband and wife got into a crowded lift and the wife was annoyed to see him pressing up against a beautiful blonde. All of a sudden, the blonde smacked him across the face, shouting,

"How dare you pinch me!"

As the couple got out of the lift the shamed husband turned to his wife and said,

"I didn't pinch her, Doris, you must believe me."

"I know you didn't," replied the wife.

The old builder was on his deathbed, the final moments ticking away.

"Marjorie," he croaked, "when I die I want you to marry Bob Higgins."

"But why?" she asked.

"Because he cheated me out of a plot of land," came the reply.

REVENGE

A woman walked into the hairdressers and said to the stylist,

"Can you cut my hair so that it's longer on one side than the other. Then can you dye it bright orange and make it go all frizzy?"

"Well, madam, I'm not sure," replied the stylist.

"You managed to last time I came in," she retorted.

Said one woman to another,

"I collect antiques, you know."

"Yes, I've seen your husband," came the reply.

Clive took a pot shot at Henry. He rubbed Henry's bald head remarking loudly,

"By jove, your head feels as smooth as my wife's backside."

Henry slowly rubbed his hand over his head and replied,

"My goodness, so it does."

REVENGE

A man was sitting despondently at the corner of the bar nursing a full pint of beer. He was about to put it to his lips when a quarrelsome 6' thug snatched the pint from his hands and drank it straight off.

"So what are you going to do about that?" said the thug challenging the poor man.

"Nothing," replied the man sadly. "I should have guessed something like that would happen to me today. First I wake up this morning to find the wife has left me and taken the kids with her. Then I'm involved in an accident and my car's a right off. So I get to work late and the boss fires me. But if that isn't enough, just as I get the nerve up to kill myself, you go and drink my last dose of arsenic."

SEA STORIES

It was the HMS Victory and only moments to go before Nelson's death. He beckoned Hardy forward and said,

"Kiss me, Hardy."

"Now he asks me," muttered Hardy, "after all this time on board!"

The night was inky black. Up ahead, the captain of the warship saw a light on collision course with his vessel.

He immediately ordered a signal to be sent saying: 'Change your course 20° east.' But the light signalled back: 'Change your course 20° west.'

The captain was furious.

'I am the captain of one of Her Majesty's warships,' he signalled, 'change your course immediately.'

'That may be so,' came the reply, 'but it is you who must change course.'

The captain was beside himself with rage. He signalled:

'Obey me! I am the keeper of the country's defences!'

'Yes, and this is a lighthouse,' came the reply.

A young woman was so depressed that she decided to end her life by throwing herself into the ocean. She went down to the docks and was about to leap into the frigid water when a handsome young sailor saw her tottering on the edge of the pier crying.

He took pity on her and said, "Look, you've got a lot to live for. I'm off to the States in the morning, and if you like, I can stow you away on my ship. I'll take good care of you and bring you food every day." Moving closer, he slipped his arm round her shoulder and added, "I'll keep you happy, and you'll keep me happy." The girl nodded yes. After all, what did she have to lose?

That night, the sailor brought her aboard and hid her in a lifeboat. From then on every night he brought her three sandwiches and a piece of fruit, and they made passionate love until dawn.

Three weeks later, during a routine inspection, she was discovered by the captain. "What are you doing here?" the captain asked. "I have an arrangement with one of the sailors," she explained. "I get food and a trip to the States, and in return, he's screwing me."

"He certainly is," replied the captain. "This is the Mersey Ferry!"

SEX

After examining his patient, the doctor said she was run down and needed rest.

"Stop having sex with your husband for a couple of months," he suggested.

"Okay," she replied. "I've got a couple of boyfriends who could stand in for him."

"Look at these," said the man enthusiastically, "they're called Olympic condoms because they come in gold, silver and bronze!"

"And what are you going to wear?" asked his wife.

"The gold, of course."

"Well it would be nice if you wore a silver one and came second for a change," she replied bitterly.

In a lecture on sexual behaviour the professor commented on a woman who'd had more than 100 orgasms in one session.

"Bloody hell," remarked one of the men, stunned, "who was this woman?"

"Oh, never mind that," retorted a woman. "Who was the male?"

There once was a nymphomaniac who lived in the land of Nursery Rhymes. She was forever out and about looking for new conquests and her behaviour was getting so bad that the Fairy Godmother came to visit her.

"You've been warned many times to stop screwing every man in sight," she said angrily, "so there's only one way to stop you," and with that she waved her magic wand and turned the girl's pussy into a pumpkin.

Some time later, the nymphomaniac returned home with a big smile on her face.

"Hi everyone," she called, "meet my new man, Peter, Peter?"

How can you tell if you're making love to a nurse, a teacher or an air hostess?

A nurse says, "this won't hurt a bit."

A teacher says, "we're going to have to keep doing this until we get it right."

An airhostess says, "now just hold this over your mouth and nose, and breath normally."

"How are you feeling?" the theatre manager asked his leading man.

"Not so good," replied the man, "I've got a terrible sore throat."

The manager took him aside and whispered in his ear.

"Listen, this may sound odd, but when I had a sore throat, my wife gave me a blow job and it cleared up almost immediately. Why don't you try it?"

"Yeah, thanks, I will," said the man gratefully. "Do you think your wife can do it for me tonight?"

A young girl walked into a hardware store and as her eyes met the old storeman's across the counter, a magic moment occurred. It was love at first sight. Within a week, the happy couple were married and spent their honeymoon on a round-the-world cruise. When they returned home, the old storeman went down to his local for a quick pint and bumped into his cribbage partner.

"Welcome home Ernie," he said "did you have a good time?"

"It was wonderful Gerald, everything was so romantic, we made love almost every night, we…"

"Really!" interrupted his friend, "to make love almost every night is fantastic at your age."

"No, no, you didn't let me finish. I was going to say we almost made love on Monday, we almost made love on Tuesday, we almost…"

"Oh Doris, guess what. I've got this complaint that every time I sneeze I have an orgasm."

"Golly, what are you taking for it?"

"Pepper."

Why does a bride smile when she walks up the aisle?

She knows she's given her last blow job.

"What sort of a week have you had?" asked the receptionist to the chambermaid.

"Well, a bit funny really. Take yesterday, for instance. The bell went for room 32 and when I went up to see what was wrong, a man pulled me inside, stripped me naked and had his wicked way with me… And the odd thing is, I never did find out why he rang the bell."

A chicken and an egg were lying in bed. The chicken was smiling contentedly and smoking a cigarette while the egg was looking depressed and tearful.

"Well, I suppose we answered that question," muttered the egg.

"I'm not feeling myself tonight," said David.

"Well that's good," replied his wife, "you can feel me for a change."

SEX

Why is sex like a game of bridge?

You don't need a partner if you have a good hand!

A young couple are on a walking holiday far away from civilization when they are lucky enough to witness a UFO landing and see two strange people emerge from the craft.

"Come on," whispers the husband, "this is our chance to be good ambassadors, let's go over and introduce ourselves."

The odd foursome spend all afternoon together learning about each other's cultures and as it gets dark, they decide to swap partners for the night to experience different sexual practices. The woman disappears with the alien man and they both strip off.

"Oh," says the woman disappointed when she sees his very small todger. But the man smiles confidently, wiggles his right ear and it grows to an enormous length."

"Ooooh!" exclaims the woman and she watches in delight as he wiggles his left ear and sees his todger thicken six times over.

The following morning, the couples meet up, say goodbye and go their separate ways.

"So how did it go?" asks the man to his wife. "Did you have a good night?"

"Fabulous," she says dreamily. How about you?"

"I don't know," he replies, "it was a bit odd, she kept trying to wiggle my ears."

75-year-old Gloria, walked into the lounge of the old people's home and said loudly,

"If anyone can guess what's in my hand, then they can have sex with me tonight."

No one answered.

"Come on" she urged "let's have some guesses."

"Okay," sighed one old man, reading his newspaper, "it's a 3-piece suite."

Everyone laughed, but the old woman thought for a moment and then said,

"Okay, that's close enough."

SHAGGY DOG

Caesar was at the peak of his popularity in Rome and much of this was due to his great warrior, Brutus. Time after time, Brutus would set out on another campaign and always come back victorious.

Each time he returned to Rome, Caesar presented him with another medal which he kept in a special chest next to his bed – Brutus loved medals and every day he would get them all out and polish them.

However, the mines that produced the gold to make the medals eventually ran out of metal.

"Brutus," said Caesar, "you are to be presented with another 5 medals but this time they will be made of chocolate."

"That's alright," said Brutus. "I will cherish them as much as I cherish all the others."

Then one tragic day, Brutus got out his medals to discover that three of the chocolate ones were missing. He ranted and raved around the house, accusing everyone in sight.

"Brutus, Brutus," said his wife gently, "you know that no one here would dare touch your medals, but I did see Caesar creeping out of here earlier this morning."

Blind with rage, Brutus high-tailed it over to the

Emperor's quarters, ran in and stabbed Caesar through the heart.

As Caesar fell to the ground, his last dying words were. 'Et tu Brutus'.

"You fucking liar," yelled Brutus, "you ate three!"

SHIPWRECKED

A man has been marooned on a desert island for 15 years. In that time he has learnt to adapt completely to his surroundings. He's built a good shelter, grown his own food and tamed some of the wild animals.

After 15 years of never seeing another human being, a beautiful young woman is washed ashore one morning, barely clothed and clinging to a small bag, containing all her worldly goods. She's delighted to see the man and is amazed at his stories of survival on the uninhabited island.

"Gosh!" she exclaims, "you're quite a man, I bet you could do with a cigarette?" The man agrees and she pulls a packet of cigarettes out of her bag and hands one to him.

As he savours the moment, she asks him if he would like a drink.

"I'd love a drink," he says. "I used to like a tot of whisky."

"Well look here," she says, and pulls out a bottle of malt whisky.

The man can't believe his luck. There he sits, smoking a cigarette and drinking the finest scotch. Moments later, the woman looks coyly at him and says,

"I guess after 15 years there's other things you haven't done either. Do you fancy playing around?"

The man jumps up with joy. "Oh no, this can't be true. Do you mean you've got a set of golf clubs in that bag as well?"

SHOPPING

A woman was examining the fruit in the grocer shop and spent some time looking closely at the cucumbers.

"Come on Madam, please," said the greengrocer impatiently. "You're not at home with your hubby now, you know. They don't get bigger the more you handle them!"

Two blonde girls walk into a department store. They walk up to the perfume counter and pick up a sample bottle. Nancy sprays it on her wrist and smells it, "That's quite nice, don't you think, Kathy?"

Kathy takes a sniff and replies, "That is nice. What's it called?"

"Viens a moi," replies Nancy.

"Viens a moi? What the heck does that mean?"

At this stage the store manager offers some help. "Viens a moi, ladies, means 'come to me' in French."

Nancy takes another sniff, then offers her arm to Kathy again, and remarks, "That doesn't smell like come to me. Does that smell like come to you?"

SHOPPING

An extremely curvaceous young woman was trying on a low cut dress and asked the shop assistant for her opinion.

"Hmm," said the assistant thoughtfully, "do you have hair on your chest?"

"Of course not!" she replied.

"Well, in that case, the dress is cut too low on you."

"I'd like a Barbie doll for my daughter," said the woman to the sales assistant "can you show me what you have?"

"Certainly madam. This is Barbie with her scuba diving at £9.50, here's Barbie dressed for the disco at £12, this is Barbie ready for the beach at £12 or there's divorced Barbie at £150."

"What!" exclaimed the woman, "why is divorced Barbie so expensive?"

"Oh that's easy to explain," replied the sales assistant, "divorced Barbie comes with the house, Ken's car, Ken's trailer and all Ken's other possessions."

SHOPPING

A pretty young woman went into the department store for some dress material and was served by a cocky young man. When she asked how much it was, he replied,

"A kiss per yard," winking at her slyly.

"OK," she replied "I'll have 5 yards."

The man cut and wrapped the material, handed it to her and said "that'll be 5 kisses please."

The young woman pointed to a wrinkly old man standing next to her,

"Grandad's paying," she said, walking away.

A woman went to the butchers to buy a chicken. She lifted it up, sniffed under one wing, sniffed under the other wing and then sniffed between the legs.

"I'm not having this," she complained. "It's not fresh."

"Madam," said the butcher impatiently. "Would you pass such a test?

SICK

Three medical students were the best of friends but one of them smoked very heavily and every morning would start the day with a terrible bout of coughing.

"You'll cough your guts up," the others would say.

One night they went out to celebrate the end of exams and came home plastered. Dave, the smoker, collapsed on the bed but the other two were still wide awake. They decided to try and put an end to his smoking. They sneaked down to the laboratory and picked up a jar of intestines which they spread all over Dave's bed. The next morning, all three arrived down for breakfast but Dave looked particularly sick.

"You alright?" one of the others asked.

"No, not really," he replied, "a terrible thing happened last night. I coughed my guts up, just as you said would happen."

"Never!" they exclaimed, "that must have been awful."

"It wasn't that so much," he replied, "it was when I had to stuff them all back in again."

SICK

The young man burst through the doors of the surgery and shook the doctor by the hand.

"Thank you doctor, thank you so much," he said. "You couldn't possibly imagine how much I've benefitted from your treatment."

The doctor looked puzzled. "But you're not one of my patients," he said.

"That's right," replied the man, "but my mother-in-law was, and I've just come from her funeral!"

SOLDIERS

The general was not a drinking man but on the occasion of the reunion dinner, he hit the brandy bottle quite seriously. In fact he drank so much, he couldn't remember getting back to his quarters.

The following morning, he woke with a blinding headache and was unable to get out of bed. At 8 o'clock his batman arrived and picked up the general's clothes which were strewn all over the room.

"I'm afraid your regimental tunic is badly marked," said the batman, holding up the jacket.

"Oh dear, yes," said the general acutely embarrassed. "Some silly chap bumped into me last time and was sick all over the front of my clothes," he lied. "When I find out the name of the bloody man, he'll be confined to barracks for the next two months."

"Well I'd make it four months, sir," replied the batman, "the bugger's also had a crap in your trousers."

The commander of the fort received a message, warning him that a massive Indian attack was imminent and he should get the men well prepared. Immediately, there was a great flurry of activity as everyone was called back to base including an old

Indian scout. Lookouts were posted and a few hours later came a shout that something was moving on the horizon.

"Tell me what's happening," the commander asked the old scout, so the Indian put his head to the ground and informed him,

"200 Indians are coming straight towards us, in the front is Running Bear and his three mighty warrior sons. They have guns as well as bows and all are painted with white stripes and four red spots across the forehead."

The commander was very impressed.

"You can even describe such small details, just by putting your head to the ground?" he asked in amazement.

"I can see under the gate," replied the Indian.

A man was posted to a remote outpost in the middle of the desert and after three months, all he could think about was sex. He needed it so much that eventually he went to see his C.O. in the hope that something could be done.

"Yeah, I can help you," replied the C.O. "There's an old traveller, lives in a tent about two miles from here, and when the men get restless, they go and see him. You get a good time down there if you spend a little money."

"Oh no!" gasped the man. "I don't go in for things like that."

However, three months on, the man was so desperate, he enquired about the traveller again.

"How much does it cost?" he asked the C.O.

£200," came the reply.

"Bloody hell, I don't call that cheap!" exclaimed the soldier.

"Well it's £50 for the old traveller and £50 each for the three men who hold him down. You see, he's not into that sort of thing either."

A general and a colonel were walking across the base and each time they passed one of the private soldiers, he would salute and the general would reply with the words 'and the same to you'.

After this had happened half a dozen times, the colonel turned to the general in puzzlement.

"Why do you always say 'and the same to you'?" he asked.

"Simple," came the reply. "I was a private once so I know what he's thinking every time he salutes someone like me."

SPORT

A professional golfer had been asked to coach a young couple who had just joined the club. On the first morning, he took them out onto the greens to assess their ability.

"Let me give you some advice," he said, "it's always worked in the past for others. When you hold the club," he said to the man, "imagine you're holding your wife's breasts, not too tight, gentle but firm. Now have a go."

The man did as he was instructed and drove the ball straight down the fairway.

"Well done," said the professional. "Now it's your turn," he said, turning to the wife. "Your grip is a little tight as well, hold the club as you would hold your husband's penis." The woman took his advice but the ball only went a few yards.

"Not to worry," said the professional, "but maybe this time you should hold the club in your hands, not in your mouth!"

The interviewer was talking to the losing goalkeeper after the match.

"So what did the manager say to you all in the dressing room?" he asked.

"Am I allowed to use swear words?" replied the goalie?

"No."

"Well in that case, he didn't say anything."

"Johnson! You're late," said the manager, standing at the door with his hands on his hips.

"Yes, sir, I'm sorry. I usually dream about my football team and wake up dead on 7.30, but this morning, they had to play extra time!"

Dad was a fanatical football supporter and his happiest day was when his son got chosen to play in the local team. For two seasons, he never missed a match until one fateful day when he slipped over on an icy road outside the ground and had to be carted off to hospital. Some time later, his wife arrived to take him home.

"Our Darren's just been on the phone," she said, "he's broken his nose, got a bad gash above his eye and stud marks all the way up his leg."

"Yes, yes," said dad impatiently, "but did they win?"

One day, when Snow White returned home from shopping she found her house had burnt down.

"Oh no!" she wailed, "where are my seven dwarfs?" She began to walk through the charred rooms calling their names when she heard a voice cry "Wales for the World Cup."

"Oh thank goodness!" she exclaimed, "at least Dopey's still alive."

Poor Morrison! He'd been with the team for nearly three years and had never moved off the substitute bench. Then one Saturday, all that looked as if it was about to change.

The match had been particularly 'bloody' and

Morrison's team had used all its substitutes except himself. Now was the chance! The manager looked towards the bench and to the lone figure.

"Shall I go on?" said Morrison eagerly.

"No, get out of the way," yelled the manager. "I'm sending on the bench."

A man walked up to the football official and asked for a ticket for the match that afternoon.

"Sorry, there isn't a match today," came the reply.

"But there must be," he argued, "there's always a match on Saturday afternoon."

"Well there isn't today," replied the official impatiently.

"Well I don't believe you," persisted the man. "You're having me on."

"Now look here, you moron, read my lips. There is no M – A– T – F – C – H this afternoon, okay?"

"But there isn't an F in match," retorted the fan angrily.

"That's what I've been trying to tell you!" yelled the official.

Barbara decided to have a few practice shots out of the green before the second round of the woman's competition took place that afternoon. She made her way up to the third green and hit a huge drive up the fairway. However, it veered badly off centre and disappeared into the trees. Ten minutes later, a course official caught up with her on the fourth green.

"Barbara dear, that was a bit of a disaster on the last green. Your ball flew through the trees and hit the windscreen of a passing motorist. It shattered the glass and caused the driver to swerve into the Colonel's driveway and dent his Rolls Royce. At the same time, a milk float coming the other way, stopped so abruptly, 32 crates of milk fell off the back and broke all over the road. The milkman had to go to hospital for stitches to a cut on his forehead. "Oh my goodness!" exclaimed Barbara. "Whatever shall I do?"

The official replied, "Well the trouble is, you're tending to hook the shot, if I were you I'd try not to bend my arm so much."

The avid football fan returned from the match looking very downcast.

"What's wrong love?" asked his wife, "wasn't it a good game?"

"The other side won by five very lucky goals!" he replied furiously.

The furious cricket captain walked over to the referee and hissed, "What would happen if I called you a fucking blind bastard who shouldn't be allowed anywhere near a cricket pitch?"

"I'd report you to the authorities and have you banned for the season," replied the referee.

"OK, but what if I just thought it?"

"Well, if you just thought it and didn't say anything, then I couldn't do much about it."

"Right," said the cricketer, smiling, "that's all I wanted to know."

THICK

"I require only three things of a man. He must be handsome, ruthless and stupid."

Dorothy Parker

Why do men like clever women?

Opposites attract.

Why do most men prefer looks to brains?

Most men see more clearly than they think.

The phone rang for the fourth time that night and the husband picked it up in a rage. He listened for a moment and then bellowed,

"How the bloody hell would I know? You want the weather centre, you berk."

"Who was that, darling?" asked his wife, innocently.

"I don't know, some twerp asking if the coast was clear. Bloody pest, that's the fourth time tonight."

A man was kneeling down, praying to God.

"Oh, Lord, thank you for giving me such a wonderful wife. Why did you make her such a good cook and housekeeper?"

"So you could love her," replied God.

"Thank you, dear Lord, and why did you make her so beautiful and young looking?"

"So you could love her."

The man smiled. "And why did you make her so kind and affectionate towards me?"

"So you could love her."

"And just one more question, Lord, why did you make her so stupid?"

"So she could love you."

THICK

Three scaffolders were moaning about their lunchboxes. The first one, a Welshman, said to the other two:

"If I have Welsh rarebit and leek sandwiches one more time, I swear, I'll jump off this ledge."

The Italian looked at his box and responded:

"Yes, it is right, if I have to eat any more anchovy pizza, I will follow you off the ledge."
Then the third man, an Irishman said, "Well now, be Jesus, if I have to face any more boiled ham and cabbage soup, count me in, lads."

So the next day, lunchtime came and the three men opened their boxes.

"Aaggh," gasped the Welshman, "leeks again" and he jumped from the ledge.

"Mama mia," cried the Italian, "pizza, pizza, pizza" and he jumped from the ledge as well.

The Irishman opened his box, saw the soup, crossed himself and followed his two mates off the ledge.

Some time later, the three wives arrived at the site to be told the dreadful news. The other scaffolders also recounted what they had heard the three men talking about.

The wives of the Welshman and the Italian cried out in pain, "If only we'd known, we'd have changed the food."

But the wife of the Irishman looked puzzled. "But I don't understand," she said. "My husband always packed his own lunchbox."

Women are more irritable than men, probably because men are more irritating.

Three men were out mountain climbing when they discovered a cave in the side of the rock face.

"Cool! Let's go and explore," said one of them.

So in they went and stumbled across an old lamp.

"Hey, look at this. Wouldn't if be funny if it was a magic lamp!"

The others laughed but suddenly stopped in amazement as the man who had first spoken, rubbed the side of the lamp and out of the spout a genie materialised.

"I am the genie of the lamp and I will grant you one wish each."

"Great," said the first man. "Can you make me twice as clever as I already am?"

"Of course," replied the genie, and immediately the man began to quote great chunks out of Encyclopaedia Britannica.

The second man was so impressed, he asked to have his intelligence increased four times. Whoosh! the next minute the man was chalking fantastic mathematical equations all over the cave wall.
Then the third man spoke:

"This is incredible. Can you make me ten times as intelligent?"

"Are you sure you want that?" replied the genie. "It might be a bit alarming for you."

"Yes, yes, I'm sure," replied the man impatiently.

So the genie granted his wish and the man was turned into a woman.

Two men are walking through the jungle, one carrying a garden shed and the other a lump of concrete.

"What are you carrying that shed for?" asked the second man.

"Well if any dangerous animals come along, I can hide in the shed and remain unharmed," he said. "So why are you carrying a block of concrete?"

The second man gave him a knowing wink and replied, "If we meet any man-eating animals, I can throw down the concrete and make a faster getaway."

Why do men drive BMWs?

Because they can spell the name.

A young man was riding a bicycle through town when he stopped to speak to his mate.

"Hello, Shaun, I didn't know you had a bicycle?"

"Yeah, I got it this morning when I was walking to work," replied Shaun. "This beautiful girl rode up to me, got off her bicycle and then stripped off until she was completely naked."

"Get away!"

"Really! She then said I could have anything I wanted, so I chose the bicycle."

"Yeah, you did right," replied his friend. "The clothes would never have fitted you."

"Professor," asked John, "how long can a man live without a brain?"

"I don't know; how old are you?" she replied.

If a man said what he thought, he'd be speechless.

A man stayed out very late drinking, staggered home and crept quietly into bed so he wouldn't wake his wife. Just as it started to get light, he woke up dying for a pee.

"Hey, Betty, there's three pairs of feet in our bed," he said nudging her.

"You daft oaf," she replied scornfully. "You can't see properly with all that booze in you. Get out and count again."

So the man went to the bottom of the bed and counted again.

"Sorry, you're right," he said. "There's only two pairs here and I can see I need my toenails cut."

Women don't make fools out of men. They only conduct the performance.

If ignorance is bliss, why aren't there more happy men?

What's the similarity between a stupid man and an intelligent man?

They both think they know everything.

A husband comes home from work to find his wife in bed with another man. He goes absolutely berserk, ranting and raving for a good few minutes. Then he rushes to the wardrobe, pulls out his rifle and sticks the barrel in his mouth.

His wife jumps up screaming, "Bob! Don't, please."

"Shut up, you bitch!" he bellows. "You're next."

Did you hear about the stupid man who divorced his wife?

He was in the maternity unit waiting for her to deliver their baby when out came the midwife to tell him he had a beautiful set of twins.

The man put his head in his hands in anguish.

"Oh, no, I never thought she'd be unfaithful to me. Our marriage is over."
"But why?" asked the midwife. "There's nothing wrong here."

"Oh, but there is," he persisted. "We only did it once so the other one isn't mine."

A world-renowned professor invented a new lie detector which not only recognised when somebody told a lie, but also kicked the offender across the room.

He spent a day testing it out on people. First through the door came a young woman who was asked what qualifications she had. She told the professor she had a first class honours degree and immediately the machine kicked her across the floor. Then an older woman of 50 years came in and when she was asked her age, she replied 31. Again the machine kicked her across the room.

"Next, please," called the professor.

This time it was a young man.

"Why don't you give me your opinion on the way you view your life?" asked the professor.

"I think..." replied the man, but before he could say any more, he was kicked across the room.

A young couple were driving down a narrow country lane when suddenly the man took a corner too quickly and ploughed into the back of a car that had pulled up into the ditch to mend a puncture.

Badly shaken, the couple got out to inspect the damage but the driver of the other car was nowhere to be seen. Then they spotted a very small man sitting cross-legged on the ground, chanting to himself.

"Excuse me," said the man, "would you happen to know where the driver of this car has gone?"

"He has gone to get help," replied the little man, "but don't go. I must thank you for setting me free. I am a genie and I was imprisoned in that car for many years but now the crash has released me, so I can grant three wishes. One for each of you and the third for me."

Immediately the man said, "I wish for a Lotus Elan, what a beautiful car!"

"Then it will be yours," replied the genie.

"And I would like a house on millionaires' row," enthused the wife.

"Then, that too, will be yours." He continued, "Now it is my turn. I would like to have my way with your wife. It is many years since I had a woman."

Appalled at the idea, but realising their wishes would not come true if they refused, the wife and genie got into the back seat of the car and down to business. Some minutes later, the genie sat back with a satisfied smile on his face and said, "By the way, how old is your husband?"

"Thirty-three," she replied, looking puzzled.

"Fancy that! Thirty-three years old and he still believes in genies!"

A man came home and caught his wife in bed with another man.

"Hey!" he shouted, "what's going on here?"

The wife retorted, "See what I mean? I told you he was stupid."

An alien came down to earth and sought out a scientist that would allow him to take some brains back to his own planet for research purposes.

"This is an ape's brain," said the scientist. "It will cost you £250."

"Very good," replied the alien. "Have you anything else?"

"Yes, this is a woman's brain and it will cost £1,000."

"OK that's fine. And just one more possibly?"

"Well, this here, is a man's brain but it will cost you £5,000."

"Goodness me! Why is it so expensive?" the alien exclaimed.

"Well, it's hardly been used," replied the scientist.

A rather stupid man is driving along in his car when it gets involved in an accident with a lorry carrying nuts and bolts. The lorry sheds its load all over the car and damages it with lots of little dents.

So the next morning, the man takes it to the garage and explains to the mechanic what has happened.

Now the mechanic is an awful practical joker and once he realises the man is a right 'Herbert', he decides to have some fun. He tells the man to take the car home, blow up the exhaust pipe as hard as he can, and all the dents will pop out.

So the man does as he's told but no matter how hard he blows, the dents remain. Just then his flat mate, another 'Herbert', comes home from work and asks what is going on. After hearing the explanation, he looks at his friend and replies scornfully, "You great dumbo, of course it won't work, you need to roll the windows up first!"

What's the difference between a man and a supermarket trolley?

A supermarket trolley has a mind of its own.

Two simple men were walking through the woods when they stumbled across an old mirror. The first one picked it up, looked in it and said, "Hey, I know that bloke."

The second one took it from him and looked in it.

"Of course you do, you daft prat, it's me."

A policeman came upon a stupid man peeing in the river.

"Stop that immediately!" he shouted, "And put it away."

So the stupid man did as he was told, but he couldn't stop himself from doubling up with laughter.

"OK, what's so funny?" demanded the policeman.

"I really fooled you this time," he laughed. "I may have put it away, but I didn't stop."

One mother-in-law said to the other:

"I would never make a fool of my son-in-law. I've always allowed him to do that for himself."

Three engineers – an electrical engineer, a chemical engineer and a Microsoft engineer – are driving along in a car. Suddenly the car stalls and stops by the side of the road. The three engineers look at each other, totally at a loss.

The electrical engineer, not knowing much about mechanics, suggests, "Let's strip down the electronics of the car and try to trace where a fault might have occurred."

The chemical engineer, not knowing much about electronics, suggests, "Maybe the fuel has become emulsified and is causing a blockage somewhere in the system."

The Microsoft engineer suggests, "Why don't we close all the windows, get out, get back in, open the windows again, and maybe it will work."

Driving to a funeral and late as usual, two brothers stop off for some petrol. Tom pays and they leave; Ben forgetting his mobile phone on the counter in the fore-court shop.

Ten miles down the road he realises what he's done, and they have to get off at the next junction and retrace their route. All the while Tom is shouting at him and won't stop telling Ben what an idiot he is.

Ben speeds into the forecourt again and leaps out of the car to grab his phone. As he does so, Tom draws breath and shouts after him, "And while you're in there, you might as well pick up my wallet, too."

The old building had fallen into such disrepair that a demolition gang moved in to raze it to the ground. Eventually, only the cellar was left and as they entered the one remaining room, they were horrified to see a skeleton in the corner. All that was left were the bones and a bright green sash, which read: 'Irish Hide And Seek Championship Finals 1949'".

What should you give a man who has everything?

A woman to show him how to work it.

"Mr Peterson, I have listened very carefully to your case," said the divorce judge, "and I have decided to award your wife £450 a month."

"Well, thank you very much, Your Honour, that seems very generous," replied Mr Peterson. "I'll try and throw a couple of quid in myself each month."

THICK

A "right Herbert" of a husband was so fed up with his wife telling him he was useless that he decided to give her a surprise. He decided to paint the bedroom. Early the next morning, after she had gone to work, he bought some paint and got down to work.

His wife returned home that evening and immediately smelled the new paint.

"Now what?" she thought. Up the stairs she went and into the bedroom to find her husband lying on the floor in a pool of sweat.

"Are you all right?" she asked, going up to him. "What are you doing?"

He gasped, "I just wanted to show you I'm not as useless as you think, so I decided to paint the bedroom."

She looked around and commented, "Well, it's very nice but why are you wearing your winter coat and your raincoat?"

"Well, it said on the directions 'for best results, put on two coats'."

My husband is so stupid, when he went to the mind reader, they gave him his money back.

A man arrives home early from work and hears strange noises coming from the bedroom. He rushes upstairs to discover his wife lying naked on the bed, sweating and panting heavily.

"What's going on?" he asks.

"I think I'm having a heart attack," she cries.

"Oh, no!" he gasps, but as he rushes back down the stairs to ring for an ambulance, he bumps into his five-year-old son.

"Daddy, daddy!" says the little boy excitedly. "Uncle Ted's upstairs in the wardrobe and he's got no clothes on."

"What!" roars the man and storms back up the stairs to the bedroom. He opens the wardrobe door and sure enough, Uncle Ted is standing there naked.

"You bastard, you bloody prat!" he screams. "How could you? There's my wife on the bed having a heart attack and all you can do is run around naked, playing hide and seek with the kids."

Giles had been shipwrecked on the desert island for more than two years and was missing female company badly. His only companions were a dog and a pig. The time came when the pig looked more and more attractive and one night, he decided to make his move. However, as he started to make his way over to the pig, he was attacked by the dog and stopped from going anywhere near it. Time after time he tried, but the ever-watchful dog would immediately start to growl, so he had to abandon his plans.

Then one day a beautiful young girl was washed up on the beach. The man took her to his shelter and nursed her back to health.

"You saved my life," she said with great feeling. "If there's anything you want in return, you only have to ask."

The man smiled broadly and replied "Oh wow! Great! Thanks a lot."

"Well, what would you like?" she whispered coyly.

"I wonder if you could take the dog for a walk," he replied.

TRAVEL

A cannibal and his son were walking through the jungle looking for food when they came across a beautiful naked woman.

"Shall we take her home to eat, dad?" asked the son.

"We'll take her home," replied dad, "but we'll eat your mother."

A woman, on holiday in Africa, meets Tarzan in the depths of the jungle. She takes one look at him and immediately falls in love with his good looks and wonderful physique.

When she discovers he lives alone she says coyly, "So what do you do about sex?"

He points to a tree where she can see a hole half way up the trunk.

"Oh goodness!" she exclaims. "I'm sure you'd much rather have this," and she lies on the ground with her legs spread wide.

Tarzan walks over and kicks her hard on the crotch.

"Owww! Why did you do that?" she asks, looking hurt.

"Me check for wasps' nests first," he replies.

A woman goes to work on an Indian reservation in Arizona and for 3 months spends her time helping to educate the young children. On her final morning, once more she sits down to breakfast with the Chief and his family and says to the Chief,

"Chief Running Bull, I've been told you have a unique memory. Can you tell me what I had for breakfast on the first day of my stay?"

"Eggs," he replies, and of course he is right. The woman returns home and it's more than ten years before she's able to return to Arizona. In the meantime she's told a lot of people about the amazing memory man but many are cynical about the question she asked. It was too easy they say, you should have thought about something more searching. So when she arrives back at the reservation, she searches out Chief Running Bull, determined to ask him a more difficult question. However, remembering her manners, she enters his teepee and first greets him by saying,

"How."

"Poached," he replies.

The flight to New York has 30 minutes flying time left when lightning hits the plane and it starts to lose altitude. As the passengers sit there dumbfounded at the enormity of what is about to happen, a woman suddenly jumps to her feet in hysterics.

"No, no!" she yells "help me, I'm too young to die."

But the next moment, she realises the futility of it all and instead says,

"Alright, if I'm going to die, then my last wish is this. Is there anyone on this plane who can make me feel like a real woman, and I mean, a real woman!"

No one moves, all the passengers are caught up in this unexpected drama, completely forgetting their own peril.

Then a voice is heard and from the back of the plane a man stands up.

"I can make you feel like a real woman," he says in a deep sexy voice. Slowly he walks towards the desperate woman, unbuttoning his shirt as he goes, revealing a perfect torso, tanned and rippling with muscles. The passengers gasp as he reaches her, the woman breathes heavily in anticipation as he extends his arm and says,

"Just run an iron over this, would you, love?"

TRAVEL

An aircraft crashed in the middle of the Australian outback, leaving fourteen badly shaken survivors. For many days they wandered through the rough scrubland but slowly each fell to the wayside until there were only two left – an elderly peer and his faithful servant.

"Bates, I can't go any further," gasped the peer. "I need water, please go and find water."

The servant disappeared into the bush and returned several hours later empty handed.

"Where's the water?" asked the peer.

"I couldn't bring it, sir," came the reply.

"Couldn't? What do you mean couldn't?"

"The river was full of giant crocodiles," whispered the servant.

"Now pull yourself together man. Those crocodiles are just as scared of you as you are of them" said the peer forcefully.

"Oh, sir," he replied miserably, "If that's right, then the water isn't fit to drink anyway."

For three months, the man had been attending French language lessons at his local night school and now he was in France to test out how well he had been taught. On the first evening he visited a small restaurant and ordered onion soup but when it arrived, he noticed a dead fly floating in it.

"Excusez moi," he said to the waiter. "Regardez, le mouche."

The waiter replied,

"Non, Monsieur. Not le mouche. La mouche."

The man was extremely impressed.

"Golly, you have got good eyesight!"

A man and his wife visited Australia for the first time and stayed at a very exclusive hotel in the outback. On their second day, they hired a jeep and drove out into the bush. To their amazement, they came across a man shagging a kangaroo. The husband was shocked that his wife had viewed such a tasteless sight, yet there was a similar situation around the next bend. Yes, another figure shagging another kangaroo!

"Come on Doreen," said the husband angrily, "that's the last time we go out into the bush, let's get back to the hotel."

To their dismay, as they turned into the drive of the exclusive hotel, they notice a man with a wooden leg masturbating at the side of the road.

"Oh John," wailed his wife. "I just want to go home."

They stormed into the hotel and demanded to see the manager.

"In the past hour we've seen two men shagging kangaroos and another man masturbating in the grounds of this very hotel. What do you have to say to that?" he rasped.

"Oh come on mate," said the manager, "have a heart. How do you expect a man with a wooden leg to be able to catch his own kangaroo?"

Out in the middle of the dense jungle, the hunting party were captured by a group of native warriors and taken back to their settlement. Turning to their guide, the hunters asked him what was going to happen to them and the answer was chilling.

"We will be ritualistically killed," said the guide, "but first they will torture us."

"What do you mean?"

"We will be made to play Luma Luma roulette?"

"Well I've heard of Russian roulette," said one of the hunters, "but what's that?"

"Each of us in turn will be ordered into the tent. Inside, six holes are cut in the side of the tent and behind each hole stands a beautiful native woman. You will then put your willy into one of the holes and the woman on the other side will suck you off."

After a moment's silence, one of the hunters spoke.

"So why is it called roulette?"

The guide replied sadly,

"Because one of the women is a cannibal."

URBAN MYTH

Yesterday I was on the Underground travelling on the Victoria line. A man of Arabic appearance got off the train and I noticed that he had left his bag behind. I grabbed the bag and ran after him, caught up with him at the top of the escalator and handed him back his bag. He was extremely grateful to me and reached into his bag that appeared to contain large bundles of banknotes. He offered me a reward, but I refused.

So he looked round, made sure nobody was looking and whispered to me:

"I can never repay your kindness, sir, but I will try to. Let me give you a word of advice for you. Stay away from Aberdeen Steak Houses." I was terrified.

"Is there going to be an attack?" I whispered.

"No, sir," he whispered back, "I went there yesterday evening – the food was awful and the dessert selection extremely limited."

VETS

A man went to the vets with his sick dog and sat in the waiting room while the animal was examined next door. Fifteen minutes later, the vet came out carrying the dog and said to its owner,

"I'm sorry, I'm going to have to put the dog down."

"Oh no!" cried the man in distress. "Why do you have to do that?"

"Because he's too heavy," came the reply.

VIAGRA

A woman walked into the chemists to enquire about Viagra™.

"Can you get it over the counter?" she asked the man at the till.

"If I take two, I can," he replied.

"Can I get you some breakfast, darling," said the woman, "if you don't want anything fried, I can get you a nice piece of fresh smoked haddock with a poached egg on top."

"No thanks," he replied. "This Viagra™ seems to have taken my appetite away."

Some time later, she asked him again.

"How about a bit of lunch. I've made some thick vegetable soup and we can have that with crusty bread."

"No thanks," he said. "I'm still not hungry."

So later still, she asked for a third time.

"Let's have some dinner. A bit of sirloin, Yorkshire pudding, roast potatoes… Doesn't that sound nice?"

"I'm sorry love, I just don't have any appetite. This Viagra™'s stopped my interest in food completely."

"Alright," she said impatiently, "but can you get off me 'cos I'm fucking starving."

A man goes to the doctor complaining that since he has been taking Viagra™, he always feels so tired. After examining him, the doctor remarks,

"Well, I can't find anything wrong with you, perhaps you'd better tell me how you spend your days."

"Okay," replied the man. "I usually wake up about 6.30, make love to the wife, doze off for a while, make love again and get up about 8 o'clock. Then after breakfast I usually make love to her again in the kitchen before going off to work. At one o'clock, I drive the four miles home, make love to the wife, have lunch then go back to work. I get home at six, make love to the wife a couple of times, have supper, make love again, pop down the pub for an hour then come back and make love on the sofa. We go to bed about 11.30, have lots more love and then go to sleep. Quite often we wake up a couple of times in the night and have more."

The doctor was dumbfounded.

VIAGRA

"Well I think I can tell you what's wrong," he said. "It's too much shagging. It's wearing you out."

"Oh really," replied the man. "For a while I thought it might be all the wanking I do in the office."

Why do they give Viagra™ to old men?

So they won't roll out of bed.

Have you heard about the new 'Viagra™ Light'?

It's for those who only want to masturbate.

WIVES

A man arrived home from work to find absolute chaos. As he walked up the garden path he fell over toys, strewn all over the ground and a broken milk bottle on the doorstep. Inside, the living room was in uproar. The two small children had up-ended the furniture and pushed over the television. The carpet had food all over it plus an overturned vase of flowers and spilt glasses of milk. The kitchen was even worse. Dirty dishes, covered every work surface, the fridge had been left open so it had de-frosted and the cat was sitting on the table eating left-over food.

"Oh no!" he gasped, turning white. He was really worried that something had happened to his wife. He raced up the stairs, two at a time and rushed into the bedroom. There, sitting up in bed was his wife, reading a book and eating chocolate.

"What's going on?" he asked. "I thought you must be ill."

"Oh no," she replied, "but when you come in every day and ask me what I did... well today, I didn't."

There was a knock on the front door and Mrs Hardcastle answered it to find a woman standing there with a collecting tin in her hand.

"Good evening," she said. "I'm collecting for a home for those inflicted with the demon drink. I wondered whether you'd like to make a donation."

"I certainly would," replied Mrs Hardcastle, briskly, "but my husband's in the pub at present. Come back when it closes and you can have him."

A woman was so suspicious of her husband that she called in a private investigator to have him followed. A few days later, she received the results.

"I'm sorry, madam," said the P.I. "but there is no doubt that your husband is having an affair. He showed the poor wife photographs of the husband with a glamorous woman and video footage of him visiting gambling casinos, exclusive nightclubs and wild all-night parties.

"I can hardly believe what I'm seeing," she gasped.

"Is it because the woman is a friend of yours?" asked the P.I.

"Oh no," she replied. "It's because I had no idea he could be so much fun."

WORKING GIRLS

A man visited a brothel in Paris and asked for the services of Monique. In return, he gave her £100. The following night he came back again and at the end of the session gave her another £100.

Now Monique was intrigued by this handsome stranger and after the third night when he gave her a further £100 for services rendered, she said to him.

"I hope I see you tomorrow, you know I look forward to our time together. In fact, tomorrow's on the house."

"Well that's mighty kind of you," replied the man, "but I'm flying back to the States tomorrow. I came to see you because I know your brother and he asked me to give you £300."

A panda escapes from his cage one night and heads for Soho where he picks up a prostitute. They go back to her place but before the main action begins, the panda eats everything in the kitchen.

"Greedy sod," thinks the prostitute, "that'll all go on his bill."

For the next few hours they do the business as agreed,

then the panda gets up and prepares to leave.

"Hey," calls the prostitute "haven't you forgotten something?"

"I don't think so" he replies.

"I'm a prostitute," she says angrily.

"And I'm a panda," he replies sarcastically.

"Look you dumb animal, in the dictionary here it says a prostitute gives sex for money. Get it?"

The panda takes the dictionary from the woman and turns to the page which describes a panda.

"Look at this," he demands.

"A panda eats, shoots and leaves," she reads.

Jack had been told by a mate that if he was ever in Liverpool he ought to look up Luscious Lil who would give him the best time of his life. So, one Saturday night he sought her out and she took him back to her penthouse flat. After stripping him and encouraging his John Thomas to stand to attention, she disappeared for a moment or two and came back with a tray of delicious sweets. First of all she covered his dick in swirls of whipped cream dribbled over some chocolate sauce, sprinkled on a bowl of chopped hazelnuts and put a cherry on top.

"Hey, what's all this?" he asked in astonishment.

"Now my darling," she whispered. "I'm going to suck it all off."

"Now wait a minute," he said quickly, "it looks so good, I'm going to suck it off myself!"

"How about a blow job," said the prostitute to the Irishman.

"Oh no, no, no," replied the Irishman, "it might affect my unemployment benefit."

Two men went to see Luscious Lil, the town's most popular prostitute. The first man came out with a silly grin on his face and said to the others.

"Wow! That was something else" he exclaimed. "What a woman! She'll do anything you want for £10 as long as you tell her in three words."

"What did you say?" he asked.

"Fuck me rigid."

The second man went in and reappeared some time later looking quite dazed.

"Bloody hell!" he gasped. "You were right. What an experience. I asked her to 'lick me everywhere'… What a woman!"

Now listening to this was an old skinflint called Jake. He decided to try Luscious Lil for himself.

"I hear you'll do anything I ask for £10 as long as I tell you in three words."

"That's right," she replied.

"And that means anything?" he persisted.

"Oh yes," she said, winking at him.

"Well in that case, decorate my house."

X-RAY VISION

A man happened to pass an old antique shop and on the spur of the moment popped inside to have a look around. On one of the top shelves, he saw an old pair of glasses and as he reached up to take them, the owner approached.

"Ah, I see you're interested in the spectacles," he remarked. "In fact they're very special glasses because when you look through them, you see everyone naked."

"Get away!" laughed the man, "that's hard to believe."
"Try them on Sir, and you will see for yourself."

So the man did, and gasped with amazement. There was the owner standing there completely naked and as he looked out of the window all the passers-by were naked as well.

"I'll have them!" he said, "no matter what the cost."

So, having purchased the unique spectacles, the man decided to go home and show his wife what he had bought, before going back to work. He arrived home, entered the house, put on the glasses and walked into the front room. Sitting on the sofa was his wife and Mr. Brown from next door, both of them completely naked.

"Hello, it's me!" he said, taking off the glasses.

But the couple on the sofa remained naked.

"Oh no!" complained the man. "£500 I paid for these, and they're knackered already!"

YETI

A group of British explorers were hunting for a Yeti in one of the more remote regions of Asia. On the fifth night, their guide told them they were very close to their target but whatever happened, they must not touch one.

"Remember my warning, do not touch the Yeti."

They made camp and settled down for the night but just before dawn, one of the explorers woke to find a huge figure looming over him. In sudden panic, he jumped up and made his escape but inadvertently touched the Yeti on his way out. He raced from the camp and down the mountainside but every time he looked round, the Yeti was coming up behind him. The explorer increased his pace and made it back to the village in a record time of 2 days. He sighed with relief, but as he turned to look back up the hillside, he could see the Yeti still following him. It was his worst nightmare. He caught a bus to the city, 60 miles away, and headed straight for the airport where he boarded the first plane for home. Arriving in London, he began to relax but as he jumped on the Heathrow Express he spotted the Yeti coming through customs. So as soon as he arrived in Central London, he raced off to Euston and took a train to the Scottish isles.

"I'm free, I'm free!" he yelled, as he stood on top of the

mountain, but alas, right behind him stood the Yeti. In complete despair, he sank to his knees and awaited his fate.

"I give up," he muttered. "I can't go on."

The Yeti approached, raised his arm and touched the man on the shoulder.

"You're it!" he said.

ZEN QUOTES

Do not walk behind me, for I may not lead. Do not walk ahead of me, for I may not follow. Do not walk beside me, either; just f*** off and leave me alone.

The journey of a thousand miles begins with a broken fan belt and a flat tyre.

It's always darkest before dawn. So if you're going to steal your neighbour newspaper, that's the time to do it.

Don't be irreplaceable; if you can't be replaced, you can't be promoted.

No one is listening until you make a mistake.

Always remember you're unique, just like everyone else.

Never test the depth of the water with both feet.

It may be that your sole purpose in life is simply to serve as a warning to others.

It is far more impressive when others discover your good qualities without your help.

If you think nobody cares if you're alive, try missing a couple of car payments.

Before you criticize someone, you should walk a mile in their shoes. That way, when you criticize them, you're a mile away and you have their shoes.

Some days you are the bug, some days you are the windshield.

ABOUT THE AUTHOR

JOHNNY SHARPE has been cracking gags since as far back as he can remember. His family call him the 'giggle machine'. Johnny's comedy show, *The Clown in Me*, was a moderate success when he launched it in County Down in 1978. Well known in his native Crawley for his highly effective practical jokes, he can often be seen chuckling as he orders his next batch of custard pies. Johnny Sharpe is single and currently on tour. He is a Saggitarius.